Please remember that this is a library book,
and that it belongs only temporarily to each
person who uses it. Be considerate. Do
not write in this, or any, library book.

The Hearing Impaired:
Birth to Six

Advisory Editor: Daniel Ling, Ph.D.

The Hearing Impaired:
BIRTH TO SIX

June Grant, Ph.D.
Professor, Director of Special Education
Trinity University
San Antonio, Texas

A College-Hill Publication
Little, Brown and Company
Boston/Toronto/San Diego

Photographs by Richard Crowther,
Instructional Media Services, Trinity University

College-Hill Press
A Division of
Little, Brown and Company (Inc.)
34 Beacon Street
Boston, Massachusetts 02108

Library of Congress Cataloging in Publication Data
Main entry under title:

Grant, June, 1920–
    The hearing impaired.

    "A College-Hill publication."
    Includes bibliographies and index.
    1. Children, Deaf—Eduation (Preschool) 2. Hearing impaired children—
Education (Preschool) 3. Children, Deaf—Language. 4. Deaf—Means of
communication. 5. Learning. I. Title. [DNLM: 1. Hearing Disorders—in
infancy & childhood. 2. Hearing Disorders—rehabilitation. 3. Language
Development. WV 271 G762h]
    IIV2430.G74   1987   362.4'2'088054   86-27402

ISBN 0-316-32402-7

Printed in the United States of America

Contents

Preface

With close to a half a century of involvement with hearing-impaired children, a lot of ideas and thoughts accumulate. Also, ideas and thoughts evolve into different patterns from their original form. Over all these years, I have observed the progress, or lack of it, among many hearing-impaired children, and have tried to account for the success or lack of it. This book makes an effort to chronicle some of these ideas in an effort to advance the quest for language facility for hearing-impaired children. If there is a single theme to the book, it is just that. Also, it focuses on only the first six years of life, for those are the most fruitful years so far as language acquisition is concerned.

The ideas expressed are not mine alone. A longtime colleague and personal friend is prominently represented in the pages that follow. Audrey Simmons-Martin and I were classmates and have had parallel years and congruous philosophies in this exciting profession. We have pooled our lecture notes, class handouts, convention presentations, workshop and seminar outlines to form the nucleus of this work. The original plan was for us to co-author this work, but the geographical distance between us and professional commitments precluded this arrangement. There are some sections that draw extensively from her unpublished outlines and presentations. The published references have been cited; her colleagues and former students will recognize her contributions readily. In addition, I have cited reported research to support our contentions, some classic studies and some recent ones involving both normally hearing and hearing-impaired children. Nevertheless, there are some assertions that I have taken the liberty to include, assertions I feel are justified from our combined long experience.

This book is for teachers and future teachers, but it is not intended to be a manual or curriculum guide. However, it is hoped that readers will glean many "generic" ideas from its pages and use the book as a starting point to develop their own philosophies and create more and more effective programs for hearing-impaired children. In the words of John Gardner, former Secretary of Health, Education, and Welfare, I hope I have offered the seeds and not the cut flowers.

The reader will infer that my instructional orientation is definitely oral–aural. However, I think all that is presented here is applicable to programs using total communication or ASL. Wherever verbal symbols are mentioned or alluded to, a sign could be inferred. After all, it is language facility I am promoting, and any language that aids the child in communication competency, cognitive activity, and creative expression serves him well.

I have used the first person pronouns throughout the book, both singular and plural. When I have used the plural, I have meant my colleagues, all teachers of hearing-impaired children. There are also many "shoulds" and "musts" in the chapters; these have been used to denote the imperative nature of the admonitions in my opinion, and for this I do not apologize.

For ease of reading only, I have used the masculine pronoun for the child and the feminine for the adult, whether a teacher or a parent. I have referred to the parent often as only the mother, again, solely for convenience. In every instance, either "mother" or "father" could be used, but to avoid the confusion of the third person pronoun, I have used the feminine, knowing full well that fathers are just as interested in and important to the welfare and education of their children as mothers are.

I have used the term "hearing-impaired" to encompass the total range of hearing deficits, from mild to profound. Where little children from birth to six are concerned, any hearing impairment can impede the language acquisition process and intervention is called for.

There is a natural progression in the book, from background and general information concerning the essence of "meaning," how children learn in general and how they learn language, and the role of parents in the learning process to the more specific areas of parent–infant programs, early childhood programs, the exploitation of creativity, and the problems faced by children from non-English-speaking homes. However, each chapter is an entity with its own theme and could be read in isolation from the rest of the text.

Lastly, I would like to thank the administration of Trinity University for granting me academic leave to get started on this project. Also, I want to express my extreme gratitude to Dr. Wallace Bruce, Director of Sunshine College School for Deaf Children, San Antonio, Texas, the teachers, staff, and the children and their parents. All have been most gracious in permitting photographing of themselves and the children during conference sessions, indoor class sessions, and outdoor play periods; they have even adjusted schedules to accommodate the photographer and me. As a teacher I can appreciate how disruptive all this can be. I am likewise grateful to Mary Esther Vasys for reading parts of the manuscript and offering valuable suggestions.

The group to whom I owe a debt that I can never repay is all the hearing-impaired children I have known over the many years, many of whom are now grown with children of their own. They have taught me so very much. But most of all, I am grateful to my husband, Harold, for his encouragement, patience, and indulgence over this protracted period of time, in addition to his invaluable editorial advice and assistance with the word processor and printer. This project could not have been completed without his Job-like endurance.

CHAPTER 1

Introduction

T he subject matter of this book is the management of hearing-impaired children from birth to age six. Not too many years ago, there was no formal "management" for children in this age group. As late as the 1960s Texas law would not allow the School for the Deaf to accept children under the age of 5 years 10 months. The influence of these early years, however, on later development has become more and more evident (Elkind, 1979; Hunt, 1980; Kagan, Kearsley, and Zelazo 1980; Uzgiris 1977; White, Kaban, Shapiro, and Attanucci, 1977, among many others). The rise of the preschool movement in the 1920s and 1930s led to the incorporation of nursery schools in some schools for the hearing impaired. Central Institute for the Deaf in St. Louis, Missouri had a well developed preschool program long before World War II, as did other schools for the hearing impaired. The greatest change in programs for hearing-impaired children, however, came with the establishment of programs for parents of hearing-impaired infants. In 1958 Central Institute initiated one of the earliest programs for this group, under the direction of Dr. Audrey Simmons-Martin. Early intervention and the technological advances in sound amplification have made a tremendous impact on the education of hearing-impaired children. These two factors have directed research and financial support to an age group that until that time had never been considered as a population to receive formal educational services.

An additional influential force in the education of hearing-impaired children has been the explosion of knowledge in the area of language

1

acquisition of normally hearing children. The evidence that the discipline of linguistics has produced showing that children learn the language of their culture in their very early months and years was one of the factors forcing educators of hearing-impaired children to extend their programs to younger and younger children. It soon became evident, however, that attenuated preschool programs could not adequately serve infants and their parents, just as watered down elementary programs cannot serve preschool children. Consequently, educators had to retool their own knowledge base and develop new skills in order to serve this new population. I have witnessed and participated in this evolution, and now I am presenting a summary of the insights gleaned from more than 40 years of experience as a teacher of hearing-impaired children and as a teacher-educator.

This volume is addressed to teachers of hearing-impaired children: inservice teachers and preservice teachers who are well advanced in their programs. It is assumed that both groups have adequate backgrounds in human growth and development, learning theory, Piagetian cognitive stages, and the language acquisition process. These fields of study are fully represented in the current literature, and to present them here in any detail would be cumbersome. Therefore, salient aspects of these subjects will be glossed only where necessary to clarify or elucidate statements. Moreover, a knowledge of the subject of linguistics and the problems hearing-impaired children encounter in acquiring language is assumed. The components of language, phonology, syntax, semantics, and pragmatics are discussed in relation to hearing-impaired children, taking for granted that the reader is conversant with these terms and the respective roles of the components in language use. The concepts of competence and performance are germane to language acquisition and use for hearing-impaired children, as are the concepts of deep structure and surface structure. These concepts are discussed in the course of the book, for they are relevant to the difficulties that hearing-impaired children encounter with language use, but the concepts themselves are not detailed.

This offering is intended to be a practical addition to the professional's library, one that can be used for reference, for reassurance, and for consideration. Theoretical aspects have been kept to a minimum. However, there is no way to anticipate every contingency that occurs in a classroom of hearing-impaired children, or in a conference with parents of hearing-impaired infants; the only way a teacher can be prepared for all the "deviations" from the expected is to have a sound theoretical basis which can be a guide in the fulfillment of long term objectives. Therefore, some basic theory has been inserted to support the ideas and practices presented. Such theoretical knowledge is the foundation for the teacher's rationale for the programs designed for the majority of students, and the adjustments made for the atypical learner or situation.

TEACHING–LEARNING PHILOSOPHY

Repeated throughout the book, both implicitly and explicitly, is the philosophy that hearing-impaired children are children first, very much like normally hearing children, and children who happen to have a handicap second. I believe that (1) the language deficit caused by the hearing impairment is the most detrimental aspect of the handicap, (2) that the most effective avenue of (re)habilitation is to create an environment whereby the child can learn language as the hearing child does, and not be taught it, (3) that the optimal time to initiate intervention is within the first months of life, (4) that the hearing-impaired child must learn to use residual hearing, no matter how minimal, through appropriate amplification and training, (5) that the total environment—the home, the intervention program, the community—has to share the same expectations for the child, and (6) that the profession is dedicated enough and advanced enough to permit hearing-impaired children to fulfill their parents' expectations and their own potential. Certain conclusions of this philosophy are not shared by all educators of hearing-impaired children. Therefore, some elucidation is called for.

NEEDS OF HEARING-IMPAIRED CHILDREN

Davis and Silverman (1978) report that there are some educators of the hearing impaired, and some deaf individuals also, who feel that the deaf are indeed different from hearing individuals, and that the hearing-impaired person should not be expected to perform in all undertakings as normally hearing people do. Myklebust (1960) has suggested that with a deficit in auditory input, a hearing-impaired child necessarily processes these stimuli differently from the manner of normally hearing children, and for that reason the former's cognitive and language development must deviate from that of the latter. It is possible that the reason hearing-impaired individuals are perceived by some educators and some deaf individuals themselves as being different is due to this modified perception, and not to significant physiological or psychological differences. On the other hand, if hearing-impaired children are perceived as no different from the normally hearing so far as basic needs are concerned, if each child is perceived as unique and not as a member of a monolithic mass, and if instruction is planned and presented with these needs as long-term goals, then it is suggested that hearing-impaired children are likely to perform in a manner similar to that of the hearing population.

Hearing-impaired children's needs as children supersede all else, but some modifications in specific areas nevertheless are required because of the handicap. Presented here are some important basic needs of children, and what few modifications are necessary to meet the needs of hearing-impaired children.

In order for any child to function meaningfully in all areas of development, a variety of factors must be considered. The child must develop physically, cognitively, emotionally, socially, linguistically, creatively, and affectively. The ability to function must include not only performing unilaterally, but performing interactionally, giving and taking in all the functions enumerated. He must be able to put sensory abilities into action, must develop and satisfy his curiosity, and must learn how to learn.

A list of a child's needs would certainly include the following:

1. To grow physically
2. To develop a healthy personality
3. To become responsible for one's own health and safety
4. To develop a positive self-image
5. To experience success
6. To communicate with the people in his ever-enlarging environment
7. To develop effective tools for learning
8. To become a contributing member of the community
9. To develop self-control and morality

Due to the sensory deficit and the concomitant language difficulty, hearing-impaired children require some extra effort on the part of their parents and teachers in satisfying their needs in all these areas.

To Grow Physically

Even though the physical needs of hearing-impaired children are no different from those of hearing children, there are some instances where caution needs to be exerted. For example, a hearing-impaired child should be able to function as a normally hearing child if the caretaker or teacher is aware of the dangers and possible complications involved when the child does not hear signals or game instructions. Adaptations to play activities are the necessary tasks of parents and teachers. The important point is that the hearing-impaired child should participate as a child with family and with hearing peers, as well as hearing-impaired peers. The child must not be a spectator.

One of the problems adults encounter with hearing-impaired children is matching physical interests with their chronological ages, taking into consideration their limited linguistic age. If a 5-year-old hearing-impaired child has the language level of an 18-month-old infant, we must match physical abilities, not linguistic age, when providing play activities. This adjustment is often difficult to reconcile, but it is important nevertheless; we must be certain that hearing-impaired children participate in the same

Figure 1–1. *Physical activity is essential for healthy growth.*

physical activities that hearing children of the same age do. Physical activity is essential for healthy growth (Figure 1-1).

Another consideration is the fact that some young hearing-impaired children may have special physical needs due to their premature births or other etiological factors. These very special physical needs, especially in the early weeks and months of their lives, and the fragility of their bodies, tend to cause parents, and teachers also, to limit the children's activities even after such limitations are no longer necessary. Also, prematurity of infants and other physical problems often have a negative effect on parenting skills. In concert with the pediatrician, parents and teachers can learn the individual child's capabilities and set the physical limits accordingly. Another special consideration for hearing-impaired children is that of the physical environment. Our students will thrive best in well lighted and sound-absorbent surroundings. Parents and teachers should strive for quiet surroundings where impact noises are at a minimum and the ambient noise level is low enough to permit speech discrimination.

If hearing-impaired children need to have their diets supplemented at school, teachers should take advantage of such an opportunity to build a teaching experience from the situation. A great deal of language can be generated while teaching the need for good nutrition.

To Develop a Healthy Personality

Every child must know that he is important to parents, family members, teachers, and others. Our usual means of expressing feelings are spoken, however, and comprehending those intonations is auditory. Even in his earliest days an infant is comforted by the sound of his mother's voice as she talks and sings. The hearing-impaired child must know that his dear ones care about him, even though he may not hear all the endearing chatter. The hearing-impaired child needs forceful assurance of affection. This means thoughtful observation on our part in order to be fully aware of his thoughts, ideas, and desires, thus enabling us to empathize with him and provide him with the expression he needs at the moment of need. The goal is a happy child who has a sense of humor, who can take correction, who has compassion and can empathize with others, and who appreciates his surroundings. These desirable traits will be reflected in the child's expressive language. Most important, we need to respect the child as an individual; this will engender self-respect that will last a lifetime. But remember that the child will not feel that he is being respected if we talk about him to others in his presence as if he were not there, or as if he could not hear us.

To Become Responsible for One's Health and Safety

Some hearing-impaired children's needs in this area appear to be greater than those of hearing children, primarily due to the impairment. The amount of greater care necessary depends upon the severity of the impairment. Our usual manner of warning a child of danger is to shout or verbally warn him. Because this channel is defective with hearing-impaired children, parents and teachers often overreact and are too restrictive in their supervision of them. Learning the strategies for getting prompt response to warnings is a task teachers and parents may have to learn from the outset. We must be consistent in our demands, and lead the children to realize that there are real dangers they need to heed when we warn them. Likewise, the child must learn from the outset to listen for warnings. For the children who cannot hear the warnings, alternate means must be employed: they can learn to watch vehicular traffic, to become sensitive to vibrations, and to note the direction to which hearing people are attending.

In the area of health, we must guard against the tendency to allow the child to remain dependent on our reminders to bathe, comb hair, brush teeth, and tend to all the matters of personal hygiene. These are admonitions for any parent, but the parent of the hearing-impaired child has additional responsibilities that should be transferred to the child at the earliest age possible. Such tasks as testing the batteries of the hearing aid, checking the cord for shorts, and cleaning the ear mold will help develop the child's independence, which is the ultimate goal.

To Develop a Positive Self-Image

Self-image begins with the child seeing himself as someone who is respected and who has the ability to think clearly and solve problems. While the normally hearing child needs a positive self-image to succeed in interactions with society, and especially to succeed in school, the hearing-impaired child needs this characteristic to an even greater extent. Not only must he be able to interact and succeed in school, but he must also develop the language necessary to maneuver the environment to his best advantage. Language being the deficient area, the child will have greater difficulty than his hearing peers, and will have to put forth greater effort to achieve success. Parents and teachers must assist the child in every endeavor in the process of building a strong self-image.

An individual's self-image has its roots in infancy, and begins to grow as parents respond immediately to the child's efforts. This parental response is extremely important with hearing-impaired children, as their vocal efforts must be reinforced promptly and affirmatively in order to guarantee repetition and establishment. The parent does this by imitating the baby's vocal efforts and encouraging vocal play. Feedback of vocalizations is one of the first steps to a positive self-image. The baby realizes that the parent is imitating him; he is delighted with this repetition; a cycle is started, and vocalization is reinforced.

Another important step in developing a positive self-image is associating one's name with oneself. As early as possible, children must be encouraged to respond to their names auditorially and to think of their names as a symbolic representation of themselves. Hearing individuals cannot remember learning their names; they (the names) have always been a part of their beings, their psyches. It should be so for hearing-impaired individuals also.

Another builder of a positive self-image is for adults to let children know that they too have the right to express emotions such as displeasure, disappointment, happiness. In this way we can help them appreciate their rights as well as ours.

To Experience Success

Successful experiences are great reinforcers of behavior and provide powerful motivation for continued activity. Very young infants experience success as they reach for and grasp an object that has attracted their attention. Such successes occur daily, and they are reinforced by the parents' praise every time the baby attains a new developmental milestone. Parents guarantee continued success by avoiding activities that are beyond the baby's ability, such as climbing stairs, before they are capable of the act. Thus, the supportive family affords an environment in which the infant succeeds in practically all endeavors.

A rule of thumb for teachers should be that every day each child should experience success in at least one activity. Continual failure can completely destroy any motivation, and a teacher must know the ability levels of all students to avoid repeated failure. An easy trap to fall into is that of teaching to the child who always knows the correct answer; every child must be an active participant. The more "troublesome" the child, the more he should be involved. The child who deserves it the least needs the most praise and love. A teacher should never tell a child a task is easy; when it is accomplished, the child feels that it was no great feat. Or even worse, if the child fails to accomplish it, he is a double failure; he cannot accomplish even an easy task. On the other hand if he thinks he is pursuing a difficult task, its accomplishment is a great achievement, and failure is more acceptable, since the task was so difficult anyway. Tasks should be carefully selected to be within the child's ability, but always with enough challenge to keep up excitement and eliminate boredom. Remember that success is self-reinforcing, and such success will help a child tolerate errors. Consider the negative reinforcement of constantly hearing statements such as, 'That's not good speech," "That's not good language," "Say it again," or "Susie, can you correct John's mistake?" We can build in success for every child in every activity with careful planning.

To Communicate with People in an Ever-Enlarging Environment

Children should feel secure in their relation with people by feeling that they are truly members of the class group. No child should be a constant spectator in the classroom or on the playground. Each needs a balanced schedule of individual teaching sessions and group participation, but should not be idle while the teacher is occupied with another child. The child needs to be a contributing member of the family group, the class group, and progressively larger groups. Such interaction is developed through many activities, such as the participation in the decisions made in all areas in which he is involved: choices of class experiences, teammates in games and other activities, food to be cooked both at school and at home, and any activity where it is appropriate for children to make decisions. Other activities which promote interaction are sharing experiences: sharing toys, sharing food, sharing stories (both fictional and true), sharing friends.

The child must be understood and understand all members of the family. The same is true in the classroom; the child must be able to communicate with all members of the class, not just the teacher. The next step is the entire school, then the neighborhood, then church associates, scout troop, and on and on to larger groups. Language must serve to communicate in all these situations, or the child's needs are not being met. This development comes naturally in most cases among normally hearing children, but teachers and parents must monitor closely the behavior and actions of hearing-impaired children to guarantee that they are indeed communicating with all members of the various groups. It is easy, unfortunately, to ignore the non-disruptive or passive child.

To Develop Effective Tools for Learning

The content of the curriculum is subordinate to the mastery of the skill of learning. Learning to learn takes top priority, not what we are teaching. This is true whether the learner is the adult (the parent) or the child. We are teachers of individuals, not teachers of facts, or vocabulary, or language structures. Facts change too fast in this highly technological society for us to require that children memorize them simply for the sake of having them at their command. Facts learned 50 years ago (such as "48 states in the United States," "92 chemical elements," "the capital of Brazil is Rio de Janeiro,") are no longer valid. Of course, some facts must be learned, but more important is the ability to sort out important ones and to learn how and where to attain them. Learning is a lifelong process which requires certain skills, and teachers and parents must help children acquire the skills. Because the hearing-impaired child has the extra burden of requiring assistance in learning language, the adults involved need to exert extra caution in selecting the topics for instruction; let us determine that everything we require the children to learn is truly useful and important.

To Become a Contributing Member of the Community

At first, the child's community is closely circumscribed, but as each new developmental milestone occurs, the child's "community' enlarges. Early on, children should develop a sense of obligation to each of their communities. Just as they have learned to communicate in various settings, they must also return the love, attention, and protection (both physical and emotional), and the productivity that the communities have provided them. Such sensitivities begin to evolve at an early age in the home, and parents must be helped in fostering their growth. Teachers must also nurture the concept in school.

The child must participate in all aspects of his community, not be just a receiver. The main tool for this interaction is language; its functional use is as an aid in the thinking process within the context of the child's membership in the various communities. In many respects, the hearing-impaired child receives more attention, instruction, and observation than normally hearing children. Care must be taken to prevent the hearing-impaired child from thinking of himself only as a receiver instead of both a receiver and a contributor.

To Develop Self-Control and Morality

The need to encourage children to exercise self-control is ever present. To control one's emotions does not necessarily mean to suppress them, and children need to know what pleases us and displeases us, as well as they need to express their own pleasure and displeasure in acceptable ways. The examples of self-control that children see, however, will be very impressive in their development of this trait. When a child observes a teacher or parent losing her temper, the child can justifiably infer that it is acceptable behavior. If a child is reprimanded for losing control of his temper after witnessing an adult doing so, he very likely will infer that when he is an adult, he can lose his temper with impunity. The examples that the teachers and parents provide will be very influential in the child's emotional development. We want our students to be able to seek long-term goals, and delay gratification in order to attain those goals.

In addition to self-control, we want to instill the concepts of justice, honesty, tolerance, fair play, compassion, empathy. Teachers must be ever alert to any prejudices or intolerant attitudes among their students. The classroom is one of the child's first experiences of working with a group other than family members, and the lessons learned there carry great influence. A teacher should not allow any child to be singled out as undesirable or incompetent or inferior to the other children. Of course, not every child will excel in every activity, but teachers can point out the balance of strengths and weaknesses of individuals. Many bits of moral and ethical behavior are transmitted from parents and teachers to children in very casual and incidental exchanges; for example, "That's not nice; I wouldn't do that." Hearing-impaired children miss out on many of these encounters. Therefore, unless attention is focused on the development of morality and ethical practices with hearing-impaired children, the growth of desirable mores may be thwarted.

SUMMARY

In summary, we find that the hearing-impaired child's needs are the same as those of normally hearing children, but fulfilling the needs are more difficult because of the hearing deficit and the concomitant language delay. The most effective way to overcome the discrepancy is for parents and teachers to concentrate their efforts on the child's acquisition of language and its functional use. Language is the prime facilitator in satisfying the needs of children, and any deficit can cause a breakdown in the progress of the fulfillment of the needs. Society is quick to inform us when we do something wrong, but not so quick to praise our positive actions. It is easy for teachers and parents to fall into the habit of reprimanding more than praising, and teachers would do well to scrutinize their presentations in terms of what is and is not being learned instead of what is being taught. What children learn has a great deal to do with their concerns, desires, interests, fears, anxieties, joys and other emotions and reactions to the world. Dealing with their inner concerns constitutes recognition of a respect for them. The experiences they have, either as a result of the reactions mentioned or as a prelude to them, are all important to them. The child and his experience are inseparable; they are one and the same. By validating these experiences and feelings we tell children in essence that they do know a great deal about the world, and that they are important. If we want to satisfy their needs, we need to assess the climate of the classroom, the home, and the community and certify that all aspects of the environment have the capability of providing for the essential needs of the children. The teaching and learning philosophy being espoused here is accordingly one where objectives are to fulfill the hearing-impaired child's needs in the most efficient and natural manner possible.

Succeeding chapters will present these topics in greater depth, and will consider the implications for teaching that arise in connection with them. The act of communication, of transmitting meaning from one individual to another, how the child learns in general and learns language in particular are investigated in the next three chapters. The anguish that parents experience and how they can become vital forces in their hearing-impaired child's language learning are detailed next. Good early education programs for hearing impaired preschoolers, and the development of children's creative talents are then explored. Lastly, the problems that hearing-impaired children from non-English-speaking homes is brought into focus.

This work offers a summary of the management of the hearing-impaired child from birth to six.

REFERENCES

Davis, H. and Silverman, S. (1978). *Hearing and deafness.* New York: Holt, Rinehart, and Winston.

Elkind, D. (1979). *The child and society.* New York: Oxford University Press.

Hunt, J. (1980). *Early psychological development and experience.* Worcester, MA: Clark University Press.

Kagan, J., Kearsley, R., and Zelazo, P. (1980). *Infancy: Its place in human development*. Cambridge, MA: Harvard University Press.

Mykelbust, H. (1960). *The psychology of deafness*. New York: Grune and Stratton.

Uzgiris, I. (1977). Plasticity and structure: The role of experience in infancy. In I. Uzgiris and F. Weizmann (Eds.), *The structuring of experience*. New York: Plenum Press.

White, B., Kaban, B., Shapiro, B., and Attanucci, J. (1977). Competence and experience. In I. Uzgiris and F. Weizmann (Eds.) *The structuring of experience*. New York: Plenum Press.

CHAPTER 2

It All Leads to Meaning

The conveyance of meaning from one mind to another pervades the daily activities of our lives, our intellectual, social, emotional, and cultural activities. An idea emanates in the mind of a speaker or writer and is transmitted to the mind of a listener or reader. The business of conveying meaning starts at birth and permeates our actions, changing only its form as we grow and develop. The exchange of meaning from one individual to another is the means by which an individual relates to the environment, assimilates the culture, and develops the concept of "self." This exchange is probably not an exclusively human trait, but among human beings it is exceedingly refined, and essential to human interrelations. We need to examine the kinds of meaning we transmit, their development, and how they are expressed, if we are to gain any insight into the total process.

Hearing-impaired children have the same capacity and instinctive need for the ability to transmit meaning, to communicate, to exchange ideas, and to relate to others. Hence, the study of meaning is appropriate for us, as their teachers, to investigate. Philosophers have long discussed and contemplated the concept of *meaning*, but suffice it to say that for our purposes we consider meaning to be something which is intended to be expressed or indicated. That is, we communicate any concept existing in the mind as a result of mental understanding, awareness, or activity. We convey thoughts, ideas, emotions; we exchange messages. How we achieve this feat is a subject we must pursue.

Language comes immediately to mind when we think of issuing thoughts or ideas. Yet there exists a myriad of nonlinguistic avenues for the transmissions of meaning from one mind to another or to many others. Pointing, gesturing, facial expressions, body posture, offering, are only a few routes, and the young child is a master at conveying meaning even before attaining any verbal language (Figure 2-1). Whatever the means, the focal issue is the imparting of meaning. The means normally functions at the unconscious level; we are generally not aware of how we impart our meaning, but are conscious only of the message. While nonlinguistic modes of conveying meaning are exceedingly effective and usually accompany linguistic modes, the latter are more commonly employed. It is not the intention here to diminish the importance or pervasiveness of nonlinguistic means of transferring meaning, but rather to investigate the linguistic.

THE DEVELOPMENT OF MEANING

Before linguistic avenues of conveying meaning can be examined, it is necessary to ferret out the sources of meaning and their development. A thorough search on this topic would be formidable and would not serve our purposes. Instead, we need simply to identify the precursors of meaning and point out their influence on the emergence of language.

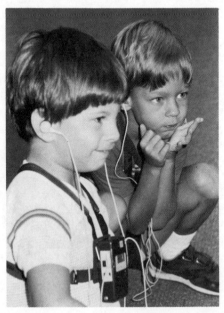

Figure 2-1. *Children can derive meanings nonlinguistically through their perceptions.*

One possible precursor is the theory that the infant probably infers the meanings of objects, rather than apprehends the objects themselves (Church, 1961). This hypothesis implies that meaning precedes actual knowledge of objects and actions. If this is so, such activity is an antecedent to the process whereby the infant uses meaning to understand the grammar of the language of his culture, not the other way around (Macnamara, 1972). Macnamara expands on his own idea stating that the above view requires a theory of how the child then brings language and thought together and how thought can be the clue to language (Macnamara, 1977).

Some investigators theorize that meanings evolve into concepts which are the requisites to language (Clark, 1977; Moerk, 1977; Nelson, 1977). Moerk summarizes the origins and development of meaning as a partially innate and partially learned phenomenon, not exclusively human, which subsequently forms the basis for concept development. This must occur before language comprehension emerges, and long before expressive language emerges. Some of the concepts that children form at the preverbal stage deal with shape, size, texture, how things move, the noise they make, and even classes or groups of entities such as agents composed of people, animals, and vehicles (Clark, 1977). The task, then, is for the child to attach linguistic symbols to the concepts in order to transmit meaning. To summarize the development of meaning in a simplistic manner: first the infant infers the meaning of objects through a possibly innate ability; then, through experiences, concepts are formed based on the already possessed meanings; and as a result of these concepts, the child attaches linguistic symbols to the concepts.

CONVEYING MEANING LINGUISTICALLY

Bearing in mind that *meaning* is the crux of this discussion, let us examine the meanings we convey (content), how we convey them (form), and the purpose (function) for which we convey them (Bloom & Lahey, 1978). If we think of language as consisting of these three aspects—content, form, and function—the area that concerns us most is that where they overlap. It is here that meaning resides. We cannot convey meaning without knowing how; we must convey our meaning in an appropriate setting and with a purpose in mind; and we must have something of import to transmit. If we trace the language acquisition process of young children, we find that they have their attention focused on meaning and use, not on structure (McNeill, 1974). In other words, they are attending to the aspect of meaning that resides in the domain of function. At the same time, parents are concerned with the accuracy of the content of what children say (Snow, 1977), and seldom correct their children for incorrect form; thus, the parents' concern is the area of meaning that resides in content. Yet neither function nor content can be effected without form, so it is necessary for us to consider all three areas as vital to the communication process.

Because function is the earliest area of language to emerge, let us examine it first. There are an infinite number of functions of language: to get attention, to convey direction, to seek information, to express feelings, to describe attitudes, to amuse others, to share opinions, to admonish and instruct oneself, to name only a few. The most frequent function of language is to communicate, however, and the function of an utterance transcends its form and content. Take, for example, the simple statement, "John kissed Mary." Those three words express an idea. The syntactic form is obvious, a simple, declarative sentence. The constituents of the sentence are straightforward; subject, verb, object, or, in semantic terms, agent, action, patient. The content, also, is straightforward; a male named John kissed a female named Mary. However, without knowing the function or intent of the speaker, the meaning is unclear; you would not know why someone would say such a thing. The speaker could be expressing surprise, informing you, making an accusation, telling a joke, telling a lie, or expressing criticism. These are all possible functions of language appropriate to that particular utterance. To decode and receive the meaning depends on more than a comprehension of the form and content. You must understand also the speaker's intent, that is, the function of this utterance. This is by no means a definitive explication of the function aspect of language, but rather a superficial definition with which to compare this aspect with the other aspects of language.

The content aspect of language is composed of thoughts, ideas, and emotions which emanate from the mind of a speaker and are received in the mind of a listener by means of a physiological act and an acoustic event. It is not a passive process. It requires a sharing of similar concepts, with a code common to speaker and listener, and a mutual understanding of the context. A sentence frequently used to illustrate the role of content is, "Mary and John saw the mountains while they were flying to California." Without an adequate understanding of the content, this could mean, "While the mountains were flying . . . ," or "While Mary and John were flying, ..." Looking up each word in a dictionary will not tell the reader that mountains do not fly. Words alone cannot convey the meaning. Rather, it is the combination of lexical meanings, and the knowledge of the world in which one lives, that is essential to the successful transmission of ideas, thoughts, and emotions from the speaker to the listener.

The form of language is the bricks and mortar of the system; the rules, the words, the sounds. To think of form as the most important aspect of language is extremely fallacious, however, for form cannot stand alone without the support of function and content. To know the sounds does not impart a knowledge of how to put them together to make words; to know the words does not include knowing how to string them together to make an understandable utterance; to know the rules does not give insight into the appropriateness of their application. For meaning to travel from one mind to another, content, form, and function must each play its role so that the message may be comprehended.

LANGUAGE BEHAVIOR AS OPPOSED TO LANGUAGE

The above oversimplified description of language indicates a necessity to distinguish *language* from *language behavior*, which is our real goal. If we wished to teach only language, our objective might be that our children know the rules of the language, have an adequate lexicon to put the rules to use, and have the skill to pronounce, write, and read the words. If, on the other hand, language behavior is our objective, the strategies and objectives would be quite different. An analogy to a card game can illustrate this distinction. The individual cards and their values are the "phonology." The set of rules of the game that one can memorize and recite is its "syntax." The "semantics" are the suits and their relative values. The game also has its "pragmatics," or the appropriate responses to the other players' actions. A player may learn all the rules of a particular game and still not play the game very well. One might say that such a person lacks "card sense." In this analogy, card sense is to playing cards what language behavior is to language; the ability to use language in appropriate ways. In the light of this distinction, let us examine again the three aspects of language, and their overlapping area where meaning resides (Simmons-Martin, 1980).

Form

With language behavior as the rubric instead of language, it is more logical to discuss the three aspects of meaning in reverse order from that which we used to discuss language. Granted, children must learn the form of their language, but they must also have opportunities to use the form in communication, in the development of concepts, in problem solving activities, and in creative expression. Situations must be structured to provide a great variety of conversational settings, rich in content, continuity, and consistency, in order for form to have the necessary context. Adult–child and child–child relations must be encouraged in discussing ideas. A caution should be injected, however, because some programs go so far in the name of spontaneity or creativity that life borders on the chaotic. Orderliness, predictability, and leisure to talk out an idea are all important for child developoment.

An exchange and exploration of ideas should begin for the

hearing-impaired child at home with parents and siblings. Parents who are not naturally highly verbal can learn to stimulate hearing-impaired children to express their ideas, to question others, to seek answers to phenomena that arouse their curiosity. Any home, no matter what the socioeconomic or educational status, is replete with activities, objects, and novelties capable of stimulating the interest of a young child. On the contrary, programs in which children only listen or act without the accompanying verbal activity, or where the teacher does most of the talking, where the teacher's language is much more elaborate than that required of the children, are programs less likely to promote positive language behavior than those that require an active role on the part of the children. Cazden (1974) reports that "in the acquisition of language use as distinct from language structure, the child is aided by what he is encouraged to say, not by what he simply hears" (p. 213). The term *language use* alludes to language behavior, and *language structure* to form. Cazden states further that adults play a major role in encouraging children to put into use what language they know, and that specific teaching of language forms can lead to learning which is too specific. If hearing-impaired children resemble normally hearing children in their comprehension of language, then we can generalize that they attend to the content of what we say, not the form (Gleason, 1973). When linguistically sophisticated parents, for example, deliberately try to teach a child a form, such as pronunciation or grammar that is too advanced for his system, the child is impervious to correction. Teachers, like good parents, need to present ideas and information about the world to children in good linguistic form, as a model.

Content

The content portion of language behavior is the "what" that we transmit from one mind to the mind of another. To return to the analogy of card playing, knowing that the nine of hearts is different from the nine of spades or the king of hearts is equivalent to the child's ability to differentiate the word *cookie* from *ball* or *milk*. For the child to incorporate "cookie" into his language behavior, he needs to have concepts similar to those of his listener. "Cookie" can be something that he wants or wants more of. It can also be baked, eaten, frosted, broken, crumbled, stacked, counted, or dropped on the floor; the child needs other concepts, as does the listener, in order that the idea, whatever it is, can be shared. The cookie might be square, round, double, or it might be chocolate, peanut butter, vanilla, frosted, and on and on. The raw material from which language grows is firsthand experiences. As Nelson (1977) states, "The child gradually builds up an experiential base of knowledge that increasingly frees him from the necessity of forming new concepts, and he becomes thereby freer to act and to think in a given situation rather than to engage in costly information processing" (p. 130).

Conceptualizing, however, is a process that never stops, and although it may result in structures (concepts) that are permanent enough to be manipulated, the process itself is a fluid one. The child applies a set of cognitive strategies which function possibly as a shortcut in the task of relating symbols to a speaker's intentions. The nature of the cognitive constraints the child uses are not known, but the work of the Gestalt psychologists on perception suggest that they are surely related to concept formation (Sinclair-de Zwart, 1971). Certainly there is also relevance to the theory of Piaget which maintains that the real objects and experiences will eventually be evoked by the word (Piaget, 1954). Concepts need to remain open and changeable as new encounters with novel experiences occur. It is not enough to categorize an animal as a "cat," because each new cat is unique. Each new experience that has not been fully predicted must be able to be modified to the child's existing concept to some extent. The modification adds a variation to the set of probable relationships. The old concepts need to be differentiated and then recombined in order to form new concepts (Nelson, 1977).

Parents assist their children in the differentiating and recombining process when they correct misconceptions such as calling a squirrel a "funny kitty." The child then differentiates cats from squirrels and recombines the common properties such as four legs, small, furry, long tail. The teacher continues in assisting the child in concept formation by programming new experiences which facilitate the development of new concepts. She encourages the children to participate actively in the planned activities, and whenever feasible, structures the experiences to entice the children to be physically engaged. A common assumption (shared by the author) is that the young child learns best through active use of the body—through participation, manipulation, and construction—rather than passive reception. Later, the active participation will be replaced by verbal and other symbolic forms, such as drawing and dramatizing.

Function

According to Vygotsky (1962), the primary function of language in both children and adults is communication or social contact. If this is the case, the child needs to have messages (meanings) to impart, and needs to have the skill to impart the messages in a manner appropriate to the occasion, considering the situation, the environment, and the listener(s). Therefore, the child needs opportunities for a wide range of experiences that lead to the development of concepts, which in turn can be related and shared. Watts (1964) expressed it particularly well, decades ago.

The difficulty, as children encounter it, is that the language required for general discussion comes easily only to those accustomed to comparing freely with one another the ideas which they have separately experienced. When experience is scanty and discussion rare, this kind of language is not readily acquired. As long as children need language merely for telling what they have seen or heard done without attempting to summarize it briefly or to express any judgment about it, they will have little or no need of words other than those which call up pictorial images of concrete things and events (p. 22).

There is no precise sequencing of what children must do to learn. They should be offered a cafeteria, not a carefully prescribed diet (Cazden, 1972). They need exposure to sentences in the context of conversations that are meaningful and sufficiently personally important enough to command attention. We need to talk with children about topics of mutual interest in the context of their ongoing work and play. To be sure, they need very specific kinds of help—help with word meanings, pronunciation, syntax, and with communicating information accurately and appropriately through language. However, the important catalyst for this accomplishment is the children's experiences and verbal interactions with their environment. They need experiences, which will in turn need labels. The ability to communicate effectively is an essential skill for all members of a culture, and the seeds for this skill need to be planted early in life and nurtured with great care and love. The implications of lack of communicative skill portend grave consequences, academically, socially, and emotionally.

Whereas communication is the most important function of language, there are others which we need to nurture, such as the use of language as a cognitive tool, and language as an avenue for creative expression. Whether language is the precursor to cognition or cognition the requisite to language, it is clear that language abilities closely accompany or parallel the development of mental abilities (Pylyshyn, 1977b). Bruner (1974) hypothesizes that the earliest use of language is a result of, and related to, an action. He states further that it is only after an action has been differentiated that the appropriate language for the action appears. This view is shared by other psychologists (Piaget, 1967; Sinclair-de Zwart 1971; Slobin, 1971a), who state that language cannot explain thought, and that after cognitive activities have been achieved, the language to accompany the activities emerges.

These views, however, do not diminish the role of language as a cognitive tool. Consider, for example, how one word can conjure up a total concept. Depending on the context, the word "water" can evoke the image of a cool drink on a hot day, the liquid in a bathtub, the contents of a lake or pond or ocean, the ingredient in a cake mix, or abstractly, the dilution of an idea, as in "to water the wine." The greater one's experience with water, the greater the number, and the more varied, the concepts evoked by the word will be. Even though the child's concepts are constantly being modified by experiences, just one word can bring to attention a complete concept whether it be composed of images, episodes, words, or whatever (Nelson, 1977).

Fowler (1977) states that language codes are the cognitive means for storing concepts, mental actions, and problem solving rules, and that oral language replaces sensorimotor action-coding to permit more complex and abstract forms of problem solving to occur. The use of language to transform a perception into linguistic form requires the organization of experiences into concepts. The linguistic structures provide the means to manipulate, store, and retrieve information at will. Language then is perceived as a cognitive tool rather than an end unto itself. Consider, also, the verbal self-direction that occurs as a child, or even an adult, attempts to solve a problem. As the task increases in difficulty, the verbalization increases also, often to the point of verbalizing aloud (Conrad, 1979). Language is an effective expedient where cognitive activity is concerned.

Language is certainly an avenue of creativity for children. Even before children are proficient language users, they engage in creative expressions. The nighttime soliloquies of Anthony Weir are an example of poetic creations by a young child, although the production of poetry was not Anthony's objective (Weir, 1962). He was indulging in verbal play, yet some of the sequences produced were highly poetic. In some respects, children are naturally poetic in their expressions. The child who spoke of himself while naked as being barefoot all over, another who described a stale piece of cake as being middle-aged, and another who intended to rise so early the next morning that it would be late, are using language as an outlet for their creativity (Chukovsky, 1968). Teachers should structure their programs to incorporate these other functions of language while they assist children in developing communication skills.

TEACHING IMPLICATIONS

How does a teacher implement a program that promotes language behavior, and not simply language? Some of the practices have already been alluded to, but further explication is in order. Our primary goal, then, is to mesh *form*, the how to say it, with *content*, the what to say, with *function*, the why, where, and to whom to say it. By meshing these the child acquires *language behavior*. These three aspects of language cannot be thought of nor taught serially or in isolation from each other; they must be thought of as a totality if we are not to vitiate the concept of language behavior. Likewise, the child's total being must be our concern, not simply many separate areas linked together. The term *global* could be applied to both the child and to the process being described here; it is a particular process that considers the total child, the code he must learn, and the context in which he learns it. Language behavior does not emerge in the child all of itself. It requires careful nurturing determined by the child's temperament, general ability, the amount of hearing, the environment, and other variables. The *whole* child is totally involved in language learning, not just the speech mechanism, the auditory system, or even the hands. The term *global* includes the memory, interests, anxieties, physical self, social development, affective stage, and cognitive level. The whole child, the global child, is to acquire language behavior.

The processes and stages that children pass through as they acquire language have been extensively investigated over the past several decades (Bloom, 1970; Brown, 1973; Dale, 1976; Jakobson, 1968; McNeill, 1970; Slobin, 1971b; to cite only a few). The discipline of psycholinguistics is replete with theories and studies that trace the acquisition of phonology, syntax, semantics, and pragmatics. However, in spite of our knowledge of what happens in the process, and when, we still are dealing with conjecture as to how this remarkable feat is accomplished.

It is interesting to note the shift of focus within the research in the field of psycholinguistics. The area of phonology had been studied and richly described as long ago as the 1940s in the work of Jakobson. However, his work was not translated into English until 1968, when other researchers became interested in linguistics due to the revolutionary work of Chomsky in 1957 (Chomsky and Halle, 1968; Jakobson, 1968; Menyuk, 1969; among others). The fact that phonology is very observable and yields to research more easily than other components of language probably accounts for its being researched earlier than the others. Its observability probably accounts also for the former preoccupation of educators of hearing-impaired children with teaching the phonology of English. The so-called "speech period" of the past consisted only of teaching hearing-impaired children to parrot sounds with little regard to meaning.

However, with the knowledge revealed by these early works, we still knew very little of how the young child learns to put thoughts into words. Some of the first detailed studies on the acquisition of language as a whole, and not phonology alone, took place in the 1960s with the entire emphasis on the area of syntax (Berko, 1958, Bever, Fodor, and Weksel, 1965; Brown and Bellugi, 1964; Brown and Fraser, 1963; Cazden, 1968; to cite some). These studies still did not reveal the secrets of what really transpires to make possible the fact that these little people, even before they have control of their bodily functions, can utter strings of words that convey meaning. Thus in the 1970s came studies that focused on semantics, or the meaning the child was imparting (Bloom, 1970; Bowerman, 1976; Nelson, 1973; to name some).

Nevertheless, the psycholinguists were not satisfied that the important facts were known, so in the later 1970s and 1980s we have had a plethora of studies on the subject of pragmatics, the uses and function of language (Bates, 1976; Dale, 1976; de Villiers and de Villiers, 1978; Moerk, 1977;

among many others). The research continues, and we still do not have all the answers, and I expect we never shall. All this research, however, does impact on the education of hearing-impaired children and how teachers and parents can enhance the language acquisition process for them.

Peters (1977) reported that both analytic and Gestalt type strategies were used by a normally hearing child. The function of the utterance determined the strategy used. Analytic speech was generally used in a referential context: naming pictures, asking for something, or labeling a quality. "Gestalt" speech, on the other hand, was used in more conversational contexts: conversations, playing, and discussing objects socially. Although the Gestalt type utterances were not as intelligible as the analytic ones, intonation factors were very prominent and length of utterance was increased. Bretherton, McNew, Synder, and Bates (1983) also point out that both analytic and Gestalt strategies are adopted by young children as they acquire language. It may be that hearing-impaired children also learn by both systems: small entries are analytically acquired, and larger ones, globally. Teachers must be familiar with all the theories and research on language acquisition so that they may use whatever it takes to plan appropriate instructional programs for their students.

The analytic theory has influenced many teachers, who seem to believe that the critical linguistic task which confronts the hearing-impaired child is learning vocabulary. With this theory as a principle, all a child should have to do to learn language is relate objects and actions in the world to their labels. Vocabulary lists of words, usually depicted in a set of pictures which remain constant over time, figure high in these programs. Progress is measured by the number of words the child can say or sign. The fallacious assumption is that the longer the list, the more language the child knows. If we reflect on vocabulary, however, this simplistic illusion disappears. Not only are there numerous names and descriptive terms which can be applied to a single object and numerous objects sharing a single name, but the terms refer to objects and actions only after having been processed through the speaker's complicated network of concepts (Pylyshyn, 1977a). How is the child who is given the word *ball* to know whether the word means shape, "rollability," "bounceability," or any other attribute? Will that child be able to attach the word to the object used on the golf course as well as the one used in a football game?

Little attention in the vocabulary approach is given to grammatical function words, which carry a large volume of meaning. For example, the articles *a* and *the* separate new information from given information, a very important factor in refining meaning. The difference between *and* and *but*, both coordinating conjunctions, is a crucial one in directing the listener's attention to the speaker's meaning. Inflections, such as third person singular "s" and past tense "ed," are powerful indicators of meaning, as are plural and possessive markers. The function words, the articles, prepositions, conjunctions, auxiliary verbs, are few in number, but frequent in use. Such linguistic forms do not name places, things, events, or actions, but express subtle relations, sometimes with diverse implications. If the content words remain constant but the function words differ, contrast the meanings among the following:

> Boy loves girl.
> What boy could love that girl?
> Many boys love that girl.
> One boy loved many girls.
> My boy loves your girl.

While it is possible to teach most content words analytically, it is impossible to teach function words that way. Since their meanings depend upon their context, they can be learned only within a context.

Other principles have permeated our pedagogy with hearing-impaired children. In fact, it has become increasingly customary in the past few decades to consider language as a code, a set of rules by which grammatical utterances are produced. The idea is that through knowing these rules, children can extract meanings, as well as produce meaningful utterances. This great concern with the surface structure of language has, in many cases, caused the important consideration of language content and function to be overlooked. In other words, the emphasis has been too great on how to say it, rather than on what to say, and why, and for whom. It is possible that our overemphasis on the separate components of the code can destroy the child's developing concept of language. Rather, we should be aware of the interrelation of conceptual understanding and the use of language in communication, cognition, and other functions, along with concern for the phonologic, morphemic, semantic, syntactic, and pragmatic principles of the verbal code. This understanding, this interrelation of all the aspects of language, is what is global. Global language, thus, is *language behavior*. It is more than the sum of all its parts; it is the intermeshing of function, content, and form.

EXPECTATIONS

It is appropriate to consider what our expectations should be if we have language behavior as our goal. While very young children can speak of only the "here and now," one goal is that they should quickly be free of this restriction. For example, we want children to be able to talk about past events, future events, abstract ideas, imaginative creations; we want them to be freed from the concrete. Another goal is that they should develop a metalinguistic awareness, an ability to think of language as an entity in itself, as well as a means of expression (Cazden, 1974; de Villiers and de Villiers, 1978). Certainly we also want children to be able to use language as a means of self-direction and logical reasoning. The development of an inner language is essential to intellectual growth.

SUMMARY

The core of our concern is *meaning*, and its conveyance from one mind to another. The natural inclination is there; as de Villiers and de Villiers state, "The child is not reciting sentence types but is conveying meanings. . ." (p. 178). Parents and teachers of hearing-impaired children can best assist them in achieving this goal by providing environments that ensure that the children develop language behavior; not form alone, not content alone, not function alone, but a coalescence of the three (Simmons-Martin, 1980). Parents of hearing-impaired children can promote this behavior with their infants and toddlers by developing good parenting skills, with the aid of professional guidance. Teachers can achieve this goal if they know the language acquisition process of normally hearing children, if they consider the temperament, the native ability, the amount of hearing, the home environment, all the characteristics of their students. In other words, what is needed is a global approach to the global child. This goal can best be accomplished when children are highly motivated to communicate, and the milieu is comfortable and nonthreatening to them.

REFERENCES

Bates, E. (1976). Pragmatics and sociolinguistics in child language. In D. Morehead and A. Morehead (Eds.), *Normal and deficient child language*. Baltimore: University Park Press.

Berko, J. (1958). The child's learning of English morphololgy. *Word, 14,* 150–177.

Bever, T., Fodor, J., and Weksel, W. (1965). On the acquisition of syntax: A critique of "contextual generalization." *Psychological Review, 72,* 467–482.

Bloom, L. (1970). *Language development: Form and function in emerging grammars*. Cambridge, MA: MIT Press.

Bloom, L. and Lahey, M. (1978). *Language development and language disorders*. New York: John Wiley & Sons.

Bowerman, M. (1976). Semantic factors in the acquisition of rules for word use and sentence construction. In D. Morehead and A. Morehead (Eds.), *Normal and deficient child language*. Baltimore: University Park Press.

Bretherton, I., McNew, S., Synder, L., and Bates, E. (1983). Individual differences at twenty months: Analytic and holistic strategies in language acquisition. *Journal of Child Language, 10,* 293–320.

Brown, R. (1973). *A first language*. Cambridge, MA: Harvard University Press.

Brown, R. and Bellugi, U. (1964). Three processes in the child's acquisition of syntax. *Harvard Educational Review, 34,* 133–151.

Brown, R. and Fraser, C. (1963). The acquisition of syntax. In C. Cofer and B. Musgrave (Eds.), *Verbal behavior and verbal learning: Problems and processes*. New York: McGraw-Hill.

Bruner, J. (1974). Nature and uses of immaturity. In K. Connally and J. Bruner (Eds.), *The growth of competence*. New York: Academic Press.

Cazden, C. (1968). The acquisition of noun and verb inflections. *Child Development, 39,* 433–448.

Cazden, C. (1972). *Child language and education.* New York: Holt, Rinehart, and Winston.

Cazden, C. (1974). Paradoxes of language structure. In K. Connally and J. Bruner (Eds.), *The growth of competence*. New York: Academic Press.

Chomsky, N. (1957). *Syntactic structures.* The Hague: Mouton.

Chomsky, N. and Halle, M. (1968). *The sound pattern of English.* New York: Harper and Row.

Chukovsky, K. (1968). *From two to five* (M. Morton, Trans.). Berkeley: University of California Press.

Church, J. (1961). *Language and the discovery of reality.* New York: Random House.

Clark, E. (1977). Strategies and the mapping problem in first language acquisition. In J. Macnamara (Ed.), *Language learning and thought*. New York: Academic Press.

Conrad, R. (1979). *The deaf school child: Language and cognitive function.* London: Harper and Row.

Dale, P. (1976). *Language development.* Chicago: Holt, Rinehart and Winston.

de Villiers, J. and de Villiers, P. (1978). *Language Acquisition.* Cambridge, MA: Harvard University Press.

Fowler, W. (1977). Sequence and styles in cognitive development. In I. Uzgiris and F. Weizmann (Eds.), *The structuring of experience*. New York: Plenum Press.

Gleason, J. (1973). Code switching in children's language. In T. Moore (Ed.), *Cognitive development and the acquisition of language*. New York: Academic Press.

Jakobson, R. (1968). *Child language, aphasia, and phonological universals* (A. Keiler, Trans.). The Hague: Mouton.

Macnamara, J. (1972). The cognitive basis of language learning in infants. *Psychological Review, 79,* 1–13.

Macnamara, J. (1977). On the relation between language learning and thought. In J. Macnamara (Ed.), *Language learning and thought*. New York: Academic Press.

McNeill, D. (1970). *The acquisition of language.* New York: Harper and Row.

McNeill, D. (1974). How to resolve two paradoxes and escape a dilemma: Comments on Dr. Cazden's paper. In K. Connally and J. Bruner (Eds.), *The growth of competence*. New York: Academic Press.

Menyuk, P. (1969). The role of distinctive features in children's acquisition of phonology. *Journal of Speech and Hearing Research, 11,* 138–146.

Moerk, E. (1977). *Pragmatics and semantic aspects of early language development.* Baltimore: University Park Press.

Nelson, K. (1973). Structure and strategy in learning to talk. *Monographs of the*

Society for Research in Child Development, 38, (1-2, Serial No. 149).

Nelson, K. (1977). The conceptual basis for naming. In J. Macnamara (Ed.), *Language learning and thought.* New York: Academic Press.

Peters, A. (1977). Language learning strategies: Does the whole equal the sum of the parts? *Language, 53, 560–573.*

Piaget, J. (1954). *The construction of reality in the child.* New York: Basic Books.

Piaget, J. (1967). *Six Psychological Studies* (Edited by D. Elkind). New York: Random House.

Pylyshyn, Z. (1977a). Children's internal descriptions. In J. Macnamara (Ed.), *Language learning and thought.* New York: Academic Press.

Pylyshyn, Z. (1977b). What does it take to bootstrap a language? In J. Macnamara (Ed.), *Language learning and thought.* New York: Academic Press.

Simmons-Martin, A. (1980). A global approach to language behavior. Paper presented at the International Congress on Education of the Deaf, Hamburg, Germany. August 4-8.

Sinclair-de Zwart, H. (1971). Sensorimotor action patterns as a condition for the acquisition of syntax. In R. Huxley and E. Ingram (Eds.), *Language acquisition: Models and methods.* New York: Academic Press.

Slobin, D. (1971a). Cognitive prerequisites of language. In W. Dingwall (Ed.), *Developmental psycholinguistics: A survey of linguistic science.* College Park, MD: University of Maryland Linguistic Program.

Slobin, D. (1971b). *Psycholinguistics.* Glenview, IL: Scott Foresman.

Snow, C. (1977). The development of conversation between mothers and babies. *Journal of Child Language, 4,* 1–22.

Vygotsky, L. (1962). *Thought and language* (E. Hanfmann and G. Vakar, Trans.). Cambridge, MA: MIT Press.

Watts, A. (1964). *The language and mental development of children.* London: G. G. Harrap.

Weir, H. (1962). *Language in the crib.* The Hague: Mouton.

CHAPTER 3

The Child Learns

How does the child learn? The scope of this topic is far too great to be treated in any depth here. Yet it is necessary to explore some different views of the learning process, the domains of knowledge and skills, and how children achieve goals, if parents and teachers are to create environments that nurture learning.

Is learning the same as development? Is development the same as cognition? Development might be thought of as a process that takes place over a protracted period of time, while learning is a short-term event (Forman and Kuschner, 1983). Cognition, on the other hand, could be thought of as being made up of the child's ever- changing concepts of the world. There is doubt that there are truly important differences among the three events, and no amount of debate can definitely resolve the issues. But the resolutions are not necessary. In the case of hearing-impaired children, the goal is for all three events—cognition, learning, and development—to occur in all aspects of growth.

The three domains of learning that require the bulk of our attention are the psychomotor, the affective, and the cognitive. The global approach to teaching and learning requires that we think in terms of all the areas if we are to provide opportunities for hearing-impaired children to exploit their full potential for learning. Any kind of learning involves brain function, and we must therefore consider the physiological aspect of learning in order to have a rationale in program planning.

Luria (1973) suggests a division of brain function into three areas: (1) an area that serves to send activating messages to the cortex; (2) the hemispheres, which obtain, process, and store information; and (3) the neocortex, which is the organizer, the integrator, the controlling element of the rest of the brain. This model presents a hierarchy, with the difficulty of the task determining the area of the brain to be activiated. Different kinds of stimuli activate different divisions of the brain. For learning to take place, all divisions of the brain must be activated.

Other models of brain functioning are of interest as they too have deep implications for teaching. Wittrock (1978) reports that the left hemisphere of the brain specializes in detail and sequence. Its storing and retrieving capabilities are analytical and often in coded form, such as words. In contrast, the right hemisphere in most people handles the Gestalt functions, perceiving wholes. Its storing and retrieving capacities appear to be more spatial, and take the form of pictures and images. One should not conclude that language is completely a left-brain function, nor that art is completely a right-brain function. Instead, the concept of the differential function of the hemispheres points out the differences in processing; that is, the two hemispheres extract different aspects of meaning from the same stimulus (Languis, Sanders, and Tipps, 1980).

Individual differences and preferences play a very important role in determining the contributions of each hemisphere in any experience. It is important for a teacher to provide freedom for children to obtain the balance that is most comfortable for them. Not only must we provide access to any combination of functioning, but we must not limit our teaching focus to only cognitive activity. We must integrate psychomotor, affective, and cognitive learning if we anticipate healthy growth. By the same token, we cannot expect the child to be an active learner in psychomotor and cognitive domains if not also developing positive affect, both in the home and at school. Hence, a healthy combination of activities that requires the interface of all three domains and stimulates responses of all parts of the brain is the setting for optimum learning (Figure 3-1).

If we think of learning as development, we then anticipate positive change. However, Kagan, Kearsley, and Zelazo (1980) warn that not all development is necessarily positive; for example, the development of a tumor, psychosis, or more commonly, a bad habit. Thus, we are not promoting change simply for the sake of change. On the other hand, the kind of change that is desirable for development is orderly, is reasonably permanent, and is judged to be of more value to the individual than the stage or process it is replacing.

It might be helpful to think of the individual stages of growth as containing elements or structures that are related to each other, and successive stages as having a relationship to previous stages, either as requisites or as competencies incorporated into the later stage. In that case, parents and teachers should make certain that current stages of development are mastered before they proceed to more advanced stages

Figure 3-1. *Outdoor play promotes psychomotor development.*

in their programs. They should ascertain that children perceive the relationship of the structures within each stage and between stages. For example, a preschool child cannot be expected to develop a concept of a week's time until he has an established concept of day and night, morning and afternoon, and now and later.

Three conditions that bring about changes in stages of development are maturation of the nervous system, acquisition of new information, and environmental demands (Kagan et al., 1980). The first of these, physical maturation, is predictable and observable. The other two, however, are capricious and subject to many influences that make generalization difficult. While acquiring new information a child will change his view of the world, as he infers meaning from new encounters. But the direction and amount of change will be controlled by his knowledge base, what he already knows. The third condition, environmental demands, is even less predictable, as each individual's environment and its influences are unique. Teachers must therefore consider each child's developmental stages on an individual basis, a judgment made by evaluating the conditions experienced by each. Such consideration is essential for maximum learning to take place.

STAGES OF COGNITIVE DEVELOPMENT

It is not possible to discuss learning and cognitive development without involving Piagetian theory. Many psycholinguists (Bates, 1976; Bloom, 1973; Bowerman, 1976; Moerk, 1977; Morehead and Morehead, 1974, among others) and psychologists (Bruner, Oliver, and Greenfield, 1966; Elkind, 1978; Flavell, 1963; Furth, 1970; Guilford, 1977; Hunt, 1961; Kagan, 1971, among others) have used Piagetian theory as the springboard for their own investigations. Therefore, a brief review of the Piagetian stages and their implications for learning, especially language learning, is in order.

Two important concepts in Piagetian theory are *assimilation* and *accommodation*. In the former, the child adjusts his perceptions of the world to make them match his internal conception of it. In the latter, he revises his internal structures in order to make sense of his new experiences in the real world (Guilford, 1977). Through continual juggling of assimilation and accommodation, the child advances from stage to stage. Each stage contains sub-stages, but we need to consider only the broad categories, and particularly the early stages.

The earliest stage is the sensorimotor period, which describes the infant's cognitive growth from birth to approximately 18 months of age. During this time, the child explores the environment through his senses and his motor capabilities. He acquires certain skills, such as coordinating hand, body, and object movements in space and time (Fowler, 1977), finding hidden objects, sitting up, skills acquired through the senses and motor abilities. One important milestone that the infant attains toward the end of this stage is the view of himself as a separate entity, apart from the rest of the objects of the world (Sinclair-deZwart, 1971). This realization, and the ability to represent actions internally, is the impetus that enables the young child to begin symbolic behavior, that is, to attach words to concepts of objects and actions (Pylyshyn, 1977). There is strong evidence that such symbolic behavior as language has its rudiments in the sensorimotor period, which is comprised of almost exclusive interaction of objects and actions (Cromer, 1976). Children must extract meaning from their actions before the actions can be expressed verbally (Languis, Sanders, and Tipps, 1980). The sensorimotor orientation lays the foundation for concept development, which in turn is the catalyst for cognitive development, which in turn is a requisite for language acquisition.

During the next stage, the pre-operational, the child engages in symbolic behavior; he learns the bulk of the grammar of the language of his culture, and he engages in pre-logical thought. Children functioning at this level are generally between the ages of 18 months and 7 years. While in this period the child is limited by his immature perceptual abilities.

The entrance into the concrete operational period is marked by the ability to use logical operations, to recognize part–whole relationships, to resolve problems involving conservation of liquids and mass, to perform reversible operations, among other capabilities. Children at this stage are usually 7 to 12 years of age.

The highest level or stage is formal operations, which is characterized by the child's ability to reflect abstractly. He can now solve problems through reflection (Ingram, 1976). Our objective, of course, is for hearing-impaired children to achieve a high level of formal operations. However, to achieve this goal, we must concentrate our efforts on the sensorimotor period, which primes the child for the next period, the pre-operational, the stage at which the important basic principles of learning in all domains are activated, and more importantly, language is acquired.

MOTIVATION FOR LEARNING

Two very powerful inducers to learning are motivation and experience. Immediately educators are reminded of the fact that there are two kinds of motivation: intrinsic and extrinsic. The former is that which comes from within the individual, and the latter, that which is forthcoming from outside the individual. An example of intrinsic motivation would be when a child (or adult) performs a task for the sheer joy of the performance or for aesthetic satisfaction, or for the thrill of creativity or any comparable reason. An example of extrinsic motivation would be when an individual performs a task for the pleasure of receiving reinforcement, verbal praise, a smile, money or other reward from an outside source. Intrinsic motivation is more effective for learning than extrinsic motivation, and the former has its roots, as does language, in the early sensorimotor period (Hunt, 1971).

Even during the first few days and weeks of life, there is evidence that the infant is motivated to respond to novel and changed perceptual stimulation. At so young an age, the kinds of experiences provided for the child determine in part how motivated he will be to seek additional stimulation. It is suggested, in addition, that the retardation and lack of activity of some infants may be due to environments that lack stimulus change. A great deal of the response during the earliest stage of life is reflexive, but in a very short time the infant exhibits a desire to maintain pleasing stimulation, showing that he is now capable of intentional behavior, not only reflexive responses. This action proves to the infant that he can make interesting things happen (Bruner and Sherwood, 1983).

The latter part in this sensorimotor period is characterized by the infant's increasing interest in novel activities, and the novel stimuli activate the child to further exploration. However, there is an optimal level of novelty that will stimulate the child, and too great a discrepancy from what the child knows will terminate the attraction (Hunt, 1971). As early as the sensorimotor period, we find a meshing of psychomotor, cognitive, and affective learning. The cognitive activity during this sensorimotor period is psychomotor in nature, and the affective aspect is influenced by the frequency, amount, and quality of the stimuli presented, and the reinforcement provided to the child. If parents provide abundant, constructive stimuli, and furnish positive, loving reinforcement, not only cognitive and affective activity are enhanced, but motivation is likewise heightened. In other words, the experiences that the environment provides for the infant have long-lasting effects on development.

Haywood and Burke (1977) offer some valuable comments on intrinsic motivation and individual differences in response to motivating stimuli. Among other ideas, they state that efficient learners, even within intelligence ranges, prefer novel, complex, surprising stimuli, whereas less efficient learners prefer more familiar stimuli. Moreover, the former group of stimuli, especially those that are slightly above the child's conceptual level, bring about an increase in tolerance of such stimuli, develop more perceptual–cognitive concepts than otherwise, and yield more efficient learning. They suggest that learning can be its own reward if the stimuli are carefully selected and are not too far above or below the child's conceptual level. They conclude that the more successful the child is in mastering explorations in this realm of new stimuli, the more pleasure he will derive and the more he will attempt new explorations. If these attempts result in continual failure, their frequency will decline. Wachs (1977) states that a child will develop at the maximum rate if he is presented with stimuli that are moderately different and not too much more complex than the stimuli that he is currently dealing with. The teaching implications of these findings are obvious; teachers must know the developmental levels of each of their students so that they may plan presentations to stimulate the students' appetites for exploration and learning.

EXPERIENCE

The role of experience is another potent factor in the learning process. The early experiences of children are considered to be very influential in their later development. The quality of the experiences has a direct effect on the child's development, as reflected in the differences in cognitive development between children from middle-class families and those from working-class families. Kagan and colleagues (1980) report that experiences of middle-class children are of a greater variety and of a more challenging nature than those of the latter group, and that middle-class children demonstrate more advanced cognitive development than working-class children.

Other researchers have found similar conditions. White, Kaban, Shapiro, and Attanucci (1977) found from a detailed and lengthy study that the children of mothers who directed language to their infants, who provided a safe environment where the children could explore and satisfy their curiosity, who served as consultants to the children, and who set limits for them, these children developed social and intellectual competence and progressed better when they entered elementary programs than children from homes where such characteristics were not present. Children who demonstrated the greatest competence at three years of age had almost twice as much social experience as those who were less competent.

Snow (1983) found that the home experiences that middle-class children have prepare them for literacy, as contrasted with children from low-income homes. The former group of children are exposed not only to books and literary materials, but also to literate features in the oral discourse that takes place in the home. Literate features, such as hearing stories from a writer's or speaker's point of view and recalling shared family events (with adults helping the children build internal representations of the events), are prevalent in middle-class homes, whereas they are frequently absent among low-income families.

Nelson's research (1973) showed that the number of outings per week that young children had—the more the better—contributed positively toward language maturity at two years of age. Another contributing factor was the number of different adults to whom the child was exposed. In other words, a multitude of varied experiences, with a variety of adults, can promote language maturity.

Another important finding is that experiences that promote development at one level may not be productive at another, later level, and may even be inhibiting (Uzgiris, 1977). Here again are important implications for teaching; experiences need to be carefully structured both at home and at school if they are to foster learning.

MEMORY

The role of memory in learning is an important one, and one that has been researched and studied by psychologists and philosophers for many years. Several topics deserve our attention, as they influence directly the learning of language for hearing-impaired children. Memory is only one of the processes a child puts into operation as he engages in various types of intellectual activity. (According to Guilford's classic study [1967], the five operations involved in intellectual activity are: cognition, memory, divergent production, convergent production, and evaluation.) Memory alone cannot support high-level intellectual activity, but it is an essential component to many forms of learning, including language.

It is not the young child's limited memory capacity that limits early linguistic utterances; rather it is the inability to organize, plan, and monitor the language rule system. The memory capacity is there, but the memory routines and strategies that would allow the child to use transformations to produce adult type utterances have not yet been developed (Olson, 1973). For hearing children, the ability to use the rule system comes naturally through hearing. In contrast, hearing-impaired children need practice in using short-term memory to represent linguistic information that eventually must be stored in long-term memory if language fluency is to come about (Figure 3-2).

Another important aspect of memory concerns the practices that promote the ability to remember. Cofer, Chmielewski, and Brockway (1975) discuss several theories on memory, but support the constructive theory, which has important teaching implications. They summarize the research that shows that how an individual remembers material is dependent upon how the material is processed, that the general idea of the input is remembered rather than the details, and that comprehension and production of the material aids the learner in drawing inferences and integrating the new material into the knowledge base. It would appear that we can aid our students in their memory tasks if we help them grasp main ideas and encourage production of the material.

Figure 3-2. *Linguistic data stored in short-term memory eventually will be stored in long-term memory.*

PRACTICE

The value of practice in the learning process cannot be overlooked, but it is often associated only with motor activities, such as riding a bicycle, playing the piano, or athletic skills. The acquisition and retention of psychomotor skills is somewhat different from the manner in which cognitive skills are acquired. While practice is an imperative factor in the acquisition of motor skills, the skills can remain for long periods without practice (Teyler, 1978). A person seems never to forget how to ride a bicycle, even after not riding for many years. Teachers of the hearing-impaired are reminded that the actual mechanical production of oral language is a motor act, and practice is an important element in the development of fluency.

Practice is also a valuable component in other forms of learning in addition to motor activities. For example, both reading and writing abilities are enhanced by practice. The more one reads, the easier reading becomes. Likewise, the most assured route to writing facility is ample practice in writing. The children who do the best writing also write in greater quantities (U.S. Department of Education, 1986). Practice is especially important for hearing-impaired children in the development of language fluency, which is a prerequisite for both reading and writing. Periods of practice must be built into any program because it is an important element in learning. But repeated, identical practice sessions can easily become boring and nonproductive. It is not an easy task for parents and teachers to contrive ways to assure practice in necessary skills without producing monotony, but it is an essential task.

There are numerous other factors to be considered when discussing how children learn, some of which are learning from models, learning by imitating, learning from one's errors, learning by attending, and learning through imagery, all of which need to be appraised in planning programs for hearing-impaired children.

MOTIVATING HEARING-IMPAIRED CHILDREN THROUGH EXPERIENCE

The young hearing-impaired child has the same capacity and same impetus for learning as the hearing child. However, he must do so with a defective auditory mechanism that impedes the language acquisition process, a most important component in the learning process of young children. Hence, the bulk of our efforts will be to enhance the language acquisition process to the greatest extent possible. As mentioned earlier, motivation and experience are major factors in any learning process, and warrant intense attention in our efforts for hearing-impaired children to achieve the language facility that will serve them in the capacities outlined above—communication, cognitive activity, and creative expression. Motivation and experience impinge on each other, and should be considered together in the planning of curricula. The kinds of experiences that the child has will be motivating or inhibiting so far as language use is concerned.

The responsibility of providing stimulating experiences falls to the parents and teachers. As pointed out by White and colleagues (1977), some parents, usually mothers in the case of young chldren, seem naturally able to design stimulating environments for their children; they appear to be able to serve as resources to the children; and they provide abundant data from which the children can infer the rules of the language. Parents who do not have these skills naturally can be helped to acquire them, and teachers need to follow the examples of the skilled mothers. However, they must not rely on instinct; they must have planned strategies to use, which will bring about the desired results. They must remember what stimulates a child: the novel, the complex, the surprising (Figure 3-3). Moreover, the stimuli are more effective if they are slightly, but not too far, above the child's functioning level. The child must experience success, and experiences that are appropriate at one level of development may not be appropriate at another level, and may even be detrimental to development.

Figure 3-3. *Classroom pets can be strong language motivators.*

Only through abundant experience will hearing-impaired children develop formal operations and be able to indulge in abstract thinking and high-order reasoning. This can be accomplished, as was demonstrated in a classroom of hearing-impaired children where the rhyme "Star Light, Star Bright" was being taught. The teacher asked a 7-year-old what she wished for. She replied, "A new bike." In contrast, an 8-year-old replied, "Many first stars." This child was on the way to seeing the higher order of things (Simmons, 1970).

In planning motivating experiences, the teacher must confront the discrepancy of the chronological age as opposed to the linguistic age of many hearing-impaired children. This discrepancy need not pose too great a problem if the teacher will consider both factors. Even though a six-year-old hearing-impaired child may be functioning linguistically at a two-and-a-half or three-year level (not too unusual a situation with many youngsters), he will not be motivated by the same stimulus that motivates the younger child. Nevertheless, an exciting experience can be structured to reconcile the difference between chronological and linguistic age. Furthermore, children at different chronological and linguistic levels can share the same experience and still attain skills and competencies appropriate to their stages.

SUMMARY

Learning takes place best when we follow the natural development of children. When teaching resists the child's built-in ability and inclinations, learning does not take place as readily nor as easily as otherwise. Programs should provide experiences that maximize the natural learning ability of children. Experiences should be varied enough to stimulate children in all domains of learning—cognitive, psychomotor, and affective. They should require processing in both hemispheres of the brain, and they should be appropriate to the child's ability and his environment. Some experiences should deal directly with the qualities and relationships of forces in the physical world; some should be mostly creative; some should be vicarious through stories, filmstrips, songs. The experiences should relate to each other and to what the child already knows, his past experiences. Through these experiences, we hope to attain intrinsic rather than extrinsic motivation for learning, interactive rather than individual problem solving, inherent knowledge rather than rote learning and regurgitative intellect, creativity and adaptive intelligence rather than task specific skills, and conceptual development through curiosity and inductive processes. With the attainment of these goals, our hearing-impaired children will be well rewarded. Bruner (1959) has reminded us that the best reward for learning is that we can use what we learn to promote thinking, and that simply learning facts is not enough.

REFERENCES

Bates, E. (1976). *Language and context: The acquisition of pragmatics.* New York: Academic Press.

Bloom, L. (1973). *One word at a time.* The Hague: Mouton.

Bowerman, M. (1976). Semantic factors in the acquisition of rules for word use and sentence construction. In D. Morehead and A. Morehead (Eds.), *Normal and deficient child language.* Baltimore: University Park Press.

Bruner, J. (1959). Learning and thinking. *Harvard Educational Review, 29,* 184–192.

Bruner, J., Oliver, R., and Greenfield, P. (1966). *Studies in cognitive growth.* New York: John Wiley & Sons.

Bruner, J. and Sherwood, V. (1983). Thought, language, and interaction in infancy. In J. Call, E. Galenson, and R. Tyson (Eds.), *Frontiers in infant psychiatry.* New York: Basic Books.

Cofer, C., Chmielewski, D., and Brockway, J. (1975). Constructive processes and the structure of human memory. In C. Cofer (Ed.), *The structure of human memory.* San Francisco: W. H. Freeman.

Cromer, R. (1976). Developmental strategies for learning. In V. Hamilton and M. Vernon (Eds.), *The development of cognitive processes.* London: Academic Press.

Elkind, D. (1978). *The child's reality: Three developmental themes.* New York: John Wiley & Sons.

Flavell, J. (1963). *The developmental psychology of Jean Piaget.* Princeton, NJ: Van Nostrand, Reinholt.

Forman, G. and Kuschner, D. (1983). *The child's construction of knowledge.* Washington, DC: National Association for the Education of Young Children.

Fowler, W. (1977). Sequence and styles in cognitive development. In I. Uzgiris and F. Weizmann (Eds.), *The structuring of experience.* New York: Plenum Press.

Furth, H. (1970). *Piaget for teachers.* Englewood Cliffs, NJ: Prentice-Hall.

Guilford, J. (1967). *The nature of intelligence.* New York: McGraw-Hill.

Guilford, J. (1977). The development of intelligence: A multivariate view. In I. Uzgiris and F. Weizmann (Eds.), *The structuring of experience.* New York: Plenum Press.

Haywood, H., and Burke, W. (1977). Development of individual differences in intrinsic motivation. In I. Uzgiris and Weizmann (Eds.), *The structuring of experience.* New York: Plenum Press.

Hunt, J. (1961). *Intelligence and experience.* New York: Ronald Press.

Hunt, J. (1971). Intrinsic motivation. In H. Schroder and P. Suedfeld (Eds.), *Personality theory and information processing.* New York: Ronald Press.

Ingram, D. (1976). Current issues in child phonology. In D. Morehead and A. Morehead (Eds.), *Normal and deficient child language.* Baltimore: University Park Press.

Kagan, J. (1971). *Change and continuity in infancy.* New York: John Wiley & Sons.

Kagan, J., Kearsley, R., and Zelazo, P. (1980). *Infancy: Its place in human development,* Cambridge, MA: Harvard University Press.

Languis, M., Sanders, T. and Tipps, S. (1980). *Brain and learning: Directions in early childhood education*. Washington, DC: National Association for the Education of Young Children.

Luria, A. (1973). *The working brain* (B. Haigh, Trans.). New York: Penguin.

Moerk, E. (1977). *Pragmatics and semantic aspects of early language development*. Baltimore: University Park Press.

Morehead, D., and Morehead, A. (1974). From signal to sign: A Piagetian view of thought and language during the first two years. In R. Schiefelbusch and L. Lloyd (Eds.), *Language perspectives: Acquisition, retardation, and intervention*. Baltimore: University Park Press.

Nelson, K. (1973). Structure and strategy in learning to talk. *Monographs of the Society for Research in Child Development, 38*(1-2, Serial No. 149).

Olson, G. (1973). Developmental changes in memory and the acquisition of language. In T. Moore (Ed.), *Cognitive development and the acquisition of language*. New York: Academic Press.

Pylyshyn, Z. (1977). What does it take to bootstrap a language? In J. Macnamara (Ed.), *Language learning and thought*. New York: Academic Press.

Simmons, A. (1970). Motivating language in the young child. In J. Utley (Ed.), *Selected readings in language for teachers of the hearing impaired*. New York: Simon and Schuster.

Sinclair-de Zwart, H. (1971). Sensorimotor action patterns as a conditon for the acquisiton of syntax. In R. Huxley and E. Ingram (Eds.), *Language acquisition: Models and methods*. London: Academic Press.

Snow, C. (1983). Literacy and language: Relationships during the preschool years, *Harvard Educational Review, 53*, 165–189.

Teyler, T. (1978). The brain sciences: An introduction. In J. Chall and A. Mirsky (Eds.), *Education and the brain. The 77th Yearbook of the National Society for the Study of Education, Part 2*. Chicago: The University of Chicago Press.

U.S. Department of Education. (1986). *What works: Research about teaching and learning*. Washington, DC: Author.

Uzgiris, I. (1977). Plasticity and structure: The role of experience in infancy. In I. Uzgiris and F. Weizmann (Eds.), *The structuring of experience*. New York: Plenum Press.

Wachs, T. (1977). The optimal stimulation hypothesis and early development. In I. Uzgiris and F. Weizmann (Eds.), *The structuring of experience*. New York: Plenum Press.

White, B., Kaban, B., Shapiro, B., and Attanucci, J. (1977). In I. Uzgiris and F. Weizmann (Eds.), *The structuring of experience*. New York: Plenum Press.

Wittrock, M. (1978). Education and the cognitive process of the brain. In J. Chall and A. Mirsky (Eds.), *Education and the brain. The 77th Yearbook of the National Society for the Study of Education, Part 2*. Chicago: University of Chicago Press.

CHAPTER 4

Learning Language

To observe a child's language emerge is an exciting experience. From the first meaningful word, perhaps intelligible only to the parents, to full discourse, is an orderly and graduated evolution. The charming utterances that often reveal the child's misconceptions are both humorous and enlightening. They tell us what the child is thinking, they give evidence of the child's growth in all domains, and they may even manipulate us. Learning language is different from other types of learning in that it takes place without apparent effort on the part of the child, and without the benefit of a "teacher." A constant reminder of this miracle arises when an adult attempts to learn a foreign language. Yet toddlers still in diapers accomplish the task with speed and ease.

We know the stages of language acquisition in young children from the plethora of literature on the subject (Bates, 1976; Bloom, 1970; Bowerman, 1979; Brown, 1973; Cromer, 1976; de Villiers and de Villiers, 1978, among others). The task of constructing a vocabulary of sounds, words, and a complex grammar on the basis of data provided by the adults and peers in the environment is the same for the hearing-impaired child as for the hearing child. The manner of receiving the data most regrettably differs.

Another disturbing difference between the normally hearing child's language acquisition and that of the hearing-impaired child is the great discrepancy in the chronological ages at which each group ordinarily advances through the stages. The experiences that motivate the hearing

2-year-old to utter two and three word sentences will not motivate the much older hearing-impaired child. However, this dilemma may be resolved with a bit of planning and forethought. To do so, we must examine the components of language to see how they may be woven into the fabric of the experiences that take place in the home and those that the teacher plans for the classroom.

Even though we are going to explore the several components of language separately, we must bear in mind the total process, the global aspect of language acquisition and the global child. This grand synthesis of phonology, syntax, semantics, and pragmatics must always be our concern as we promote language acquisition in the home and at school. The implication here is that the discrete components never occur in isolation in spoken language, and therefore should never be taught in isolation. Hence, it seems inappropriate, even incongruous, that a separate person or time can be assigned to teaching language or speech.

We can glean some insights into teaching strategies for hearing-impaired children by reviewing what the hearing child does. He or she learns, with no observable effort, to use the complex patterns of all the components of language that linguists attempt to describe with the terms phonology, syntax, semantics, and pragmatics.

THE COMPONENTS OF LANGUAGE

Phonology

The development of phonology, the acoustic reality of language, the actual sounds we hear and say, is the first component of language to appear as the child develops, and has been closely observed by linguists (Edwards, 1974; Ferguson and Garnica, 1975; Jakobson, 1968; Winitz, 1969, among other).

Whereas there is some disagreement among the theorists as to the precise sequence of the emergence of distinctive features, intonation, and other parameters of phonology, there is enough agreement for us to make some generalizations and to consider the implications for hearing-impaired children. One of the earliest features to emerge is the ability to perceive intonation patterns. By 8 months of age, an infant can discriminate between falling and rising intonation patterns such as occur in statements and some question forms (Morse, 1974). (Rising intonation is present only for yes-no questions, not for *wh* questions.) Intonation contours of English involve much more than simple rising and falling patterns, but the fact that children are responsive to intonation at such an early age is indicative of the importance these patterns play in conveying meaning.

Certainly the area of intonation has definite implications for teachers of hearing-impaired children. Consider, for example, how much meaning we can help children convey and comprehend when we teach them to attend to, to reproduce, and eventually to use intonation patterns in their meaningful communication. The punctuation of spoken language is available to the child with even a minimal amount of residual hearing. Even the young hearing-impaired child can express meaning with a single syllable by changing the prosody. Three different meanings can be interpreted from a nonsensical utterance such as "dududu"; a simple statement, a question ("dududu?"), and an exclamation requiring immediate attention ("dududu!"). Intonation is a readily available and effective vehicle for hearing-impaired children to use in their struggle to understand others and be understood. By providing correct models in their spoken language, teachers can help a child incorporate appropriate intonation patterns in his own utterances.

Another equally important component of phonology is the phonemes themselves, and how they are distinguished from each other both receptively and expressively. As early in life as 4 months, infants have demonstrated the ability to perceive the differences between various phonemic categories and voice onset time (Eimas, 1985). Whether this is accomplished in normally hearing children by developing distinctive features or by imitating the sounds that they hear is not important for our purposes; we can use both strategies in instructional programs. What is relevant to us is the process and the possibility of hearing-impaired children's emulating the process. One prevalent feature in young children's early phonology is deletion. They delete component consonants in consonant clusters, and they delete final consonants. They also substitute voiced consonants for unvoiced ones, and the other way around; they substitute stops for fricatives and vice versa; they prefer front consonants to back ones, substituting the former for the latter; and they substitute glides for liquids (Ingram, 1979).

A third feature of early phonology is the tendency to produce all vowels or consonants of a word in the same location; for example, all front vowels if the first vowel of a word is a front vowel. Other important facts are that these errors seem not to be random, but rather rule governed, and that phonemic perception precedes phonemic expression (de Villiers and de Villiers, 1978). Teachers of hearing-impaired children should remember as they select targets for speech improvement programs that their pupils may be making perfectly normal developmental errors in their articulations. This is not to disparage the teaching of phonemes, as speech intelligibility is a primary goal of our programs. Nevertheless, perfect articulation is not the sole factor in achieving intelligibility; intonation plays a strong supportive role (Hudgins and Numbers, 1942; Subtelny, 1977). Therefore, it is not a question of choosing either phonemes or prosody that confronts us, but rather the evening of the two into an effective communication process.

Syntax

In spite of the several decades of investigation on the acquisition of syntax, there is still no widespread agreement on the details of the process. However, most psycholinguists would agree on some broad concepts: that little children are limited in what they are able to say due to their limited cognitive abilities (Bloom, 1973); that they acquire fourteen elementary morphemes in a rather fixed sequence (Brown, 1973); that the early stages are completed in a relatively short period of time, with children eventually separating deep structure from surface structure; and that the knowledge of interrelationships among sentence types evolves during the early stages (de Villiers and de Villiers, 1978).

Historically, teachers of hearing-impaired children have been frustrated by their meager success in teaching word order and the cryptic use of function words. As long ago as last century, there appeared reports in the literature describing "systems," which teachers could use to aid their students in structuring their utterances. The Wing Symbols, the Barry Five Slates (cited in Moores, 1982), and later, the Fitzgerald Key (1949) were such attempts. These early researchers, and later ones, too, have sought ways to develop that combinatorial skill whereby the children could convey their meanings in acceptable, intelligible form. Possessing language facility involves the ability to form new combinations of words, grammatical classes, and sentence patterns. It is through such manipulations that we create sentences, dialogue, discourse. Except for social amenities, every sentence a person utters and every sentence a person hears is novel, unique, and creative.

Such is not the case with hearing-impaired children for the most part. Worse yet is the fact that often what we teachers say to our our students falls into the category of "rubber stamping." When 53 of 54 hearing-impaired children express a situation in precisely identical grammar—"There is a boy and a girl. They had an idea"—we need to evaluate the novelty, the uniqueness, the creativity of the data that the teachers are providing the children (Simmons, 1965). We might conclude that hearing-impaired children are functioning with impoverished data, that they do not receive adequate input to infer rules of word order, to solve the puzzle of function words (especially prepositions) or to tease out multiple meanings of words. They have limited information with which to deduce that changing the word order of "The boy hit the ball" to "The ball hit the boy" yields an entirely different meaning, that "in a minute" does not put anything "in" something, or that "on the bus" does not mean on top of the bus, that "poor thing" does not imply poverty or destitution and the "thing" in this case is usually animate. The only way hearing-impaired children can learn these structures and functions is by multiple contacts in natural contexts, as hearing children encounter them.

Semantics

The development of semantics is a complicated affair even for normally hearing children. Three aspects of early semantic development make it an ongoing and especially arduous task for hearing-impaired children. These are (1) expressing relationships among objects and actions and actors, (2) expressing propositions, and (3) acquiring the actual words and their meanings. Examples of relationships would be an agent–action–object, such as "Baby eat dinner," or a location or possessor utterance, such as "Baby sit table." Some early propositons that children express are requests, denials, references, and descriptions (Bloom, 1970; Bruner, 1983). In order to express any relationships or propositions, however, the children have to know the words and their meanings (de Villiers and de Villiers, 1978). Teachers of hearing-impaired children at times have become so preoccupied with the learning of words, the last of the three components of semantics, that the other components are often overlooked. Vocabulary is the least stable component of language; it is an ongoing process throughout an individual's life. We must be sure that the words that we provide for our students will enable them to express the semantic relationships, the requests, the denials, the references, and descriptions that young children commonly express. Certainly the young hearing-impaired child has similar ideas, desires, and questions to express.

It is doubtful how valuable it is for the hearing-impaired child to learn lists of words, even in categories, if they are presented out of context. It is not difficult for children to learn proper names, words like *Daddy, Mommie,* and the child's own name, for these names are charged with emotion and affect and thus are easily learned. Common nouns are somewhat more difficult because they apply to a whole class of objects, the members of which share properties. The child's perceptual categories probably assist in this task (Nelson, 1974), but the adult use of the word may differ from the child's meaning, and this discrepancy will require that the child modify his classification or create another category. For example, if a child's first meaning of the word *dog* is the specific family pet, he will have to enlarge his classification when he hears other quite different looking animals called *dog*. The first meaning for the word *match* may be the implement used to start a fire, an object that his parents have cautioned him about. When the word is used to mean that two things are equal or similar, the child will have to form a new classification. Simple verbs and adjectives present the same problem as nouns for a child, and the hearing-impaired child most likely will need assistance in the clarifying of these meanings.

Still harder than the groups just described are the relational words, such as *big, little, tall, short,* the meanings of which can be comprehended only through their relation to another object or standard. The confusion is amplified when the same soccer ball is little relative to the big beach ball, but is big compared to the golf ball. Even more difficult are the deictic expressions that point out or indicate an object without mentioning it. Such words as *here, there, this,* and *that,* locate an object in relation to the speaker, and their meanings can change as the speaker changes position. The same is true of the deictic expressions of time—*yesterday, today, tomorrow, this afternoon, tonight* (de Villiers and de Villiers, 1978). There is no way the hearing-impaired child can gain understanding of these very important, frequently used words except in natural context. The semantic component of language is actually the linguistic counterpart of the child's conceptual framework. He has concepts before he has the words to label them, but it takes careful mapping to match the words to the correct concepts.

Pragmatics

Pragmatics, the latest component of language to attract the attention of the researchers, concerns the context in which sentences are uttered and comprehended. Pragmatics argues that an utterance cannot be explicated out of context unless the speaker's intentions and the listener's understanding are available (Bruner, 1978). Intentions can be expressed in many different forms. An individual may make a request by asking a question, such as, "Is there any coffee left?" The intention of that speaker was not to gain information, but to make a request, and a fluent user of the language would interpret that question as just that. A speaker may ask a question by issuing an imperative, "Tell me where I can find. . . ." The degree of politeness that such an utterance might command will depend again on the context: who the inquirer is and who is to respond; which of the parties is older; which of the parties is more prestigious; which of the parties might be frustrated or angered by a preceding incident. In other words, the utterance is not interpretable without the context.

There are other important aspects to the pragmatics of language. One that facilitates or impedes conversations is the use of articles. Even very young children are able to use the correct article in their discourse, using the indefinite *a* for the undesignated noun and *the* for the already known one (Cazden, 1972). Failure to discriminate between the two is a common fault in both the oral and written language of hearing-impaired children, and such failure can cause serious breakdowns in the communication process. Many compositions of hearing-impaired children begins "The boy. . ." or "The house. . ." Part of this confusion may be the result of the teaching technique of using pictures as the stimulus for a composition. In such a case, the child is thinking of a specific, designated boy or house and assumes the listener or reader shares this knowledge. Another pitfall using pictures is the naming of objects or persons by pictures and always preceding the noun with the indefinite article; for example, *a ball*. This practice leads the hearing-impaired child to infer that these nouns are always preceded by the indefinite article, which of course is not the case. Normally hearing children naturally develop a sensitivity to their listener's perspective; what knowledge their listener has on the subject being discussed, and how much information must be provided in order for the listener to follow the conversation and yet not be bored with information that he already has.

Another skill that even very young children who are only beginning to put words together to form sentences have is that they will modify their utterances when they realize they are not being understood (Levelt, Sinclair, and Jarvella 1978). They develop these sensitivities without tutelage from their experience with language. This skill would be a valuable asset to hearing-impaired children.

Hearing children also learn how to take turns in conversations and how to ask and answer questions that facilitate the conversation without delaying it. Children as young as two to four years of age demonstrate these conversational skills, picking up many cues from intonation contours (de Villiers and de Villiers, 1978). Such a skill would be very valuable for hearing-impaired children, since they are often not understood during their conversations.

An additional important aspect of pragmatics is the ability to change speech styles for different listeners. Adults use different intonation, vocabulary, and syntax for different audiences. They speak differently to their family members and intimates from the way they speak to their friends and acquaintances, from the way they speak to their business and professional colleagues, from the way they would make a public address. While no one expects young children to possess all these levels of speech styles, young hearing-impaired children must learn that they are expected to speak differently to adults from the form of speech they use with their peers. They must learn that a child should not ask a woman her age even though that is often the first question she asks a child. Just as hearing children do, hearing-impaired children must possess different speech codes and know which listener requires a more formal or polite code; they must recognize that some listeners will need more information for background than, say, their parents or teachers, and they must have enough vocabulary to activate the different codes.

METALINGUISTIC AWARENESS

Metalinguistic awareness is not exactly a component of language, but it is certainly an important ability that enhances the language acquisition process. This ability, the capacity to think about language, its form, meanings, and uses, is present in children at a very early age and increases in its complexity from self-corrections and rephrasings to comments on the speech of others, to questions about language, to comments on one's own speech, to the ability to answer questions about language (Slobin, 1978). A four-year-old demonstrated that he was acutely aware of word meanings and their social implications when he announced to his parents that he would not tell a secret because this secret was not the kind one whispered in someone's ear; it was the kind that one *doesn't* tell.

Clark (1978) traces the development of metalinguistic awareness through six stages: monitoring one's ongoing utterances; checking the results of an utterance; testing the reality of the utterance (does it say what the speaker really means); deliberately trying to learn new sounds, words, sentences; predicting the consequences of using inflections, words, phrases, or sentences; and reflecting on the product of an utterance. The teacher of hearing-impaired children helps students monitor their own speech and helps them practice sounds, words, and sentences. Unfortunately, our students are usually engaged in these exercises at a much later age than are normally hearing children. Teachers need to help the students find ways to check the results of their utterances, to see if their listener has understood them or not, and if not, to find another way to express the idea. They must learn to decide whether or not a word really says what they mean. They need to role-play, using different speech codes for different listeners— little children, their parents, or the pediatrician. They need to know how to make rhymes, tell jokes and puns, and ask and solve riddles. Activities such as these make hearing and hearing-impaired children aware of language and its capacity for communication, socialization, and just plain fun.

STAGES OF LANGUAGE ACQUISITION

The linguistic data available to hearing-impaired children is different from that of the normally hearing child. Some of the factors influencing the amount and quality of the data are the degree and age of onset of the hearing-impairment, the age at which audiological and educational intervention occurred, the extent to which the child makes use of the residual hearing, the pattern of linguistic stimulation in the home, the parents' expectations, and the child's intelligence and motivation. As much as we endeavor to emulate the language acquisition process of normally hearing children, there will be differences due to these factors.

Because there are requisite environmental and auditory conditions for language learning, the hearing-impaired child's sensory experiences must be constantly mediated with the appropriate language code. He must be given a model to imitate, and from that imitation receive sensorimotor feedback which, in turn, can make it possible for him to progress through the stages of language acquisition of normally hearing children. Regrettably, hearing deprivation forces the development to occur at a later chronological age than normal hearing allows. Nevertheless, when children have learned to make maximum use of their hearing, when parents are instructed in ways to maximize the home experiences, and when their teachers perform the role that mothers play when young children are acquiring their language, hearing-impaired children can approach the stages that linguists consider to be universal among children with no impairment.

Whereas there is disagreement among the researchers concerning the child's innate propensity to acquire language (Bruner, 1983; McNeill, 1970), teachers of hearing-impaired children must believe that their students are endowed with the same potential capacities as other children. All teachers of long experience can attest to congenitally and profoundly hearing-impaired adults who have complete command of the language, proving that the ability is there. We need only to find the way to make it happen for all hearing-impaired students. We must be certain that the child receives the necessary data, so that he can eventually infer the principles of the grammar of the language. The data, however, must be programmed in a systematic form so that the child can advance from stage to stage (although he will do it at a later chronological age, and will remain at each stage for a longer period of time than the hearing child).

Stage I.

Chomsky (1957) was the first to hypothesize that the human infant is predisposed to acquire a language. We assume this ability exists whether the child is hearing-impaired or not. The language may be a verbal one, a gestural one, a manual one, or any combination thereof. The only reported cases where children have acquired no language are those in which the children had no opportunity to communicate with other human beings; for example, the wild boy of Aveyron (Lane, 1976) and Genie (Fromkin, Krashen, Curtis, Rigler, and Rigler, 1978). Both normally hearing and hearing-impaired children whose parents are hearing-impaired and communicate in American Sign Language (ASL) or other sign systems acquire sign language in a fashion very similar to the sequence followed by children learing oral language (Bellugi and Klima, 1972; Goldin-Meadow and Mylander, 1984; Schlesinger and Meadow, 1972). Similar strategies and mistakes occur in the two situations. The implication here for hearing-impaired children is that they will acquire whatever language they are exposed to. It is for teachers and parents, then, to provide the linguistic input of preference to the children at the earliest stages of development.

The corollary to the fact that a human child will acquire language is the time frame: this phenomenon occurs very early in life and at a rapid pace. The bulk of language acquisition occurs by the time the child is four years of age (McNeill, 1970). This does not mean that a child can acquire no language after this time period has elapsed, but it implies that language learning after this period is likely to be more difficult and less efficient. This fact alone emphasizes the need for early intervention if the normal process is to be emulated.

At this early stage, the hearing-impaired child is very much like his normally hearing peers; he gestures, he points, he communicates almost as well as any child. The responsibility here for teachers and parents is for this behavior to be encouraged and intensified. The child must know that what he has to communicate is important to the meaningful people in his life. He must be stimulated to communicate by objects and activities that are of high interest to him. Expensive equipment is not necessary to satisfy this need. On the contrary, anyone who has had experience with very young children has witnessed a young child's indifference to an array of expensive toys change to excitement and amusement with a commonplace plastic container or some such mundane household item. What is important is to seize the interest of the moment and initiate a "dialogue" with the child concerning that item that is exciting to him. The goal is communication, and at this stage, it will have to be about people or things that are immediately present; the child does not yet have the means to engage in symbolic activity.

The language acquisition process probably starts at birth, for mothers talk to their infants from the day they are born, sometimes in very sophisticated language as if the child could understand what she is saying (Cohen, Caparulo, and Wetstone, 1981). If parents do not suspect deafness, and if the baby is healthy physically, parents of hearing-impaired infants do the same as all parents.

At this time, the child only vocalizes, and the vocalizations are reinforced by the parents' responses. Parents of infants tend to speak to their babies to get their attention, or for the parents' own amusement. Therefore, their utterances are not short, syntactically and semantically simple, well formed and repetitive, as they will be after the child begins to produce words (Brown and Bellugi, 1964; Phillips, 1973). The child now is most likely processing only intonation patterns (Lewis, 1951). At this point the infant's vocalizations reflect his state of being: hunger, boredom, pleasure, fatigue, and other sensations. The mother responds by imitating the baby's cooing and gurgling, and the baby imitates the mother; they reinforce each other's vocalizations (McCormick, 1984). The prompt reward for using his voice to communicate leads the child to use phonation further, which becomes a basis for further language learning.

At this time, unless the hearing-impaired child is watching the mother and finds her utterances visually interesting, the baby does not reinforce the mother by repeating her vocalizations and the reciprocal process is terminated. Unwittingly, the mother stops her vocalizations because she is not being reinforced by the infant. In some instances, other subtle negative changes in mothering practices occur which affect the infant's preverbal communication, which is the rudiment of symbolic functioning (Galenson, Kaplan, and Sherkow, 1983). At this point, even when electronically aided, the linguistic environment of the hearing-impaired child now deviates from that of the hearing child; the degree of deviation depends on the severity of the impairment, the configuration of the impairment, the mother's reaction, and all the other factors that influence the language learning of these children. Special care must be taken at this time to provide a model for the child to imitate, and to reinforce most positively the first attempts at vocalization. The child needs to discover that he can manipulate his world through phonation. Just using his natural pleasant voice must gain some strong reinforcers, such as attention, both verbal and sensory, a hug, a kiss, whatever.

The teacher or parent should contrive situations in which the language code in its complete form can be presented for the child to process through the sensorimotor mechanism. The child's attention is on the immediate activity, but it is for the adult to supply the linguistic data to accompany the event. The adult is aware of the child's current linguistic ability and should know how to respond to the child's efforts. Critical to this procedure is the child's receiving feedback from attempts at imitation and the adult's acceptance of his best efforts. Contrived experiences should be appropriate to the child's chronological, social, and cognitive age. In some cases, the child will be an infant, in others, a toddler or preschooler. The teacher or parent must reconcile the difference between linguistic age and other measures of growth. The complete code needs to be given to these experiences, not just the lexical vocabulary or any other portion of the linguistic form (Figure 4-1). In as much as the child and the teacher or parent have performed the activities together, the linguistic form has significance and takes on meaning. The child perceives the deep structure, the meaning, and stores it in the short-term and then his long-term memory.

Stage II

During the second stage, parents label things in the child's environment. These are the things the child sees, tastes, feels, smells, hears, and does. In other words, the child's functioning is strictly sensorimotor, and the language used to label his acitivites reflects this stage. The objects and actions are very much in the child's perceptual range, in the here and now, but the child still is not labeling the objects and actions independently. His babbling now mimics the intonation patterns of the utterances of the adults around him (de Villiers and de Villiers, 1978). Parents of children at this age will often answer the question, "Does he talk yet?" with "Yes, but we don't know what language he's speaking." The children seem to

Figure 4-1. *Children learning the verbal labels for food and drink in a natural setting involving their senses.*

be asking questions, making statements, giving commands, and making requests, but in a language of unintelligible jargon. The prosodic patterns give us the punctuation and the pragmatic intent of the utterances. Like Lewis's hearing children (1963), hearing-impaired children respond and imitate affective patterns first, sentences which relate to their feelings of surprise, happiness, or dissatisfaction. If these utterances are captured and restated, they can usually be imitated easily. At the very least the prosody of the utterance can be imitated.

The teaching implication is that the adult must be sensitive to what it is that the child wishes to express, and must give vocal form to the child's feelings and intentions. Through the teacher, the preschooler gets his orientation to the kernel sentence. Instead of the stereotyped simple sentences

> We went to the store,
> Tom bought a balloon,
> Jane bought a comic book,
> Bill bought some bubble gum,

sentence groups that maintain the integrity of the child's thoughts and likewise take note of the affective domain are better:

Jane found a penny.
Oh, she was happy.

Tom bought a balloon.
It popped.
He cried.

Jack pushed a boat.
Bill got all wet.
He didn't like that.

The intonation of the sentences presented by the adult stands the best chance of carrying meaning for the child when the sentences are presented following a shared experience. Even though the child cannot read, being exposed to the printed word helps to call attention to sounds he does not hear. In this way, he discovers that something belongs in those empty auditory spaces. However, the greatest attention will be paid to intonation, which is the adult's prime objective at this stage. The child's reward for imitation of adult intonation must be acceptance of the imitation, no matter how crude, if it is the child's best effort. The reward for spontaneous use of intonation is comprehension by the adult.

Stage III

In the next stage, the adult, parent or teacher, moves on to sentences that focus more on ideas than on objects and actions. The adult adjusts the input to the child's knowledge of language (Bloom and Lahey, 1978). The parents tell about what will happen or talk of things past. "We're going to Grandmother's this weekend;" "We had fun at the park yesterday, didn't we?" With input of this type, the child is receiving information about the notion of time and how we express it. He is learning how Mother feels about things from the intonation of her voice. He is being exposed to pronouns, with their abstractness. He is getting vocabulary in meaningful context, not just the words *Grandmother, park, fun*. He is taking in the function words, *to, this, at,* which carry no meaning except in context. It is important that the complete linguistic structure be given to the child, and the parent or teacher can do just that (Newport, Gleitman, and Gleitman, 1977).

It is also important that the meaning of the sentence should grow out of a shared experience. It is at this stage that the input from the parents should be simplified, well formed, and repetitive, as it was not in the very early stage. In addition, much of the imput should be about the child himself, who is just now beginning to name objects and actions. Nouns are the most prevalent appearing, but verbs and adjectives also occur. These are the words that have primary stress patterns in the mother's model.

Sometimes the child inserts real words into meaningless utterances, signifying that he knows that other forms should be inserted, but for one reason or another does not or cannot make the additions (Bloom, 1973). While his efforts sound like jargon, the child is employing another linguistic form, rhythm, in the utterances. Imbedded in the jargon are words, but the salient feature to the listener is the prosody of the utterance.

Hearing-impaired children at this third stage should be asked to match the "time envelope" of the adult's model (Figure 4-2). Hudgins and Numbers pointed out as long ago as 1942 that the intelligibility of the speech of hearing-impaired children is reduced because of its arrhythmic characteristics. They reported that phrasing was slow and labored. It is unfortunate that in spite of all the technological advances of the past few decades, most teachers of hearing-impaired children would still agree with

Figure 4-2. *Child imitating the adult's model, with special attention to the time envelope.*

this assessment. Calvert (1962) found the deaf to take three to four times as long to articulate each phoneme as hearing children, and the relative duration between phonemes was distorted. Black (1971) found similar distortions in the length of time required by hearing-impaired children to utter a word as compared to normally hearing children. As the child works to match the time envelope of the adult's model, he is limiting breath and articulatory motion, giving better articulation as a result. If he needs units shorter than a complete sentence, the adult needs to break the utterance into phrases, but not single words. The total sentence naturally will be repeated once more for the child to perceive the rhythm and the intonation of the whole.

Stage IV

The child begins to produce telegraphic utterances in Stage IV. Characteristic of telegraphic utterances is the omission of function words, words that do not themselves make reference. They carry secondary stress and low acoustic power. The words that are likely to appear are the content words, mostly nouns and verbs that are essential to the situation. Telegraphic speech is likely the result of limited knowledge and memory (deVilliers and deVilliers, 1978). During this period, the parent's or teacher's speech to the child is still simplified, direct, and even repetitive, the kinds of utterances that the child will be producing in a year or two. For the same reasons that the normally hearing child does not attend to the function words, the hearing-impaired child likewise omits them. These words are especially unavailable to him due to their lack of stress and low acoustic power. Therefore it is extremely important that these words have representation in written form so that the child can see the words which occur in these auditory blank spaces.

When hearing-impaired children reduce their imitations of the adult's model, or when they telegraph their own spontaneous language, the adult must expand and fill in the appropriate function words, *in, of, but, so,* and others, thereby demonstrating the proper use of structural words and their meanings. In a classroom situation, in addition to the little words, the teacher's instruction should be structured in such a manner that the children begin to see that the phonemes are the building blocks of the language code. Now, the teacher puts emphasis on production of the sounds, remembering to keep the light touch, bearing in mind always that even hearing children have not mastered all the phonemes at this stage. However, rhythm, stress, and duration must constantly be monitored, since they enhance poorly articulated speech; even well articulated speech that lacks good rhythm, stress, or intonation can be tiresome to listen to and even unintelligible.

Stage V

By the fifth stage, the parent is now using causal relations, contingencies, time, and other abstract notions in utterances with the child, and the child begins to use longer sentences, to ask questions, and to gain control of a multitude of transformations (Menyuk, 1969). Although the time of acquisition of language skills varies enormously between deaf and hearing children, the sequence in categories, nevertheless, is similar. Hearing-impaired children, though generally older, follow the same sequence as normally hearing children (Kretschmer and Kretschmer, 1986). The parents' and teacher's responsibility here is to build into the hearing-impaired child's language the many dimensions of the complex language code.

The emergence of complex sentences is a case in point. Hearing children begin to comprehend and use complex sentences at approximately three years of age. The first utterances using more than one verb are of the object complement type (Bowerman, 1979), for example, "I like to read, I want to play." Hearing-impaired children seem to be able to incorporate utterances of this type into their expressive language without too much difficulty. However, the more complicated complex forms, which for hearing children quickly follow the easy forms, are not so evident in the utterances of hearing-impaired children. Conjunctions, such as *so, when, if, or, but, while, before,* and *after,* and relative clauses present great problems and require a great deal of exposure before they are mastered (Russell, Quigley, and Power, 1976). Even hearing children have some difficulty with the time conjunctions *before* and *after* (Clark, 1971). They tend to process sentences in chronological order regardless of the meaning of the conjunctions. For example, the sentence, "Before you eat lunch, wash your hands," would be processed by a young child as, "Eat lunch, wash hands," the exact opposite of the adult meaning. Adults need to be sensitive to the child's level of comprehension so that the linguistic input can affect positively the linguistic progress and not create confusion.

Normally hearing children continue to acquire more complex linguistic forms even during the stage of concrete operations. Because their cognitive development is still progressing during this stage, it is not surprising that the accompanying language must reflect these changes (Karmiloff-Smith, 1979). On the other hand, the difficulties that pre-operational children have with tasks of conservation may be partially due to their incomplete concepts of terms like *more than, thicker than, longer than* even though these terms appear in their lexicons. Thus it is imperative that hearing-impaired children acquire basic concepts and the appropriate linguistic labels through their early experiences so that they may continue to progress both cognitively and linguistically in later developmental stages. It appears that children use strategies in encoding and decoding language, but how they attain the strategies is unknown (Cromer, 1976). Because these processes are not revealed to us, the best chance the hearing-impaired child has to acquire good language is to follow as closely as possible what the normally hearing child does.

SUMMARY

The learning of language is for most children a natural and fast moving process beginning at a very young age. Unfortunately, for hearing-impaired children it is an arduous and often incomplete process, with some children never achieving fluency. Educators of hearing-impaired children can aspire to higher levels of fluency when the natural process is emulated as closely as possible. All the components of language must be meshed into a global process. The phonology, the syntax, and the semantics must combine with the pragmatics to serve the child's needs for communication, cognitive activity, and creativity. Each of these components will be augmented as the child advances from one stage to the next. Bruner (1983) states that the three facets of language—syntax, semantics, and pragmatics—are learned interdependently, and could not be learned independently of each other. Teachers of hearing-impaired children must be constantly guided by this concept as they assist their students in this process that will affect their cognitive, affective, and creative efforts all their lives.

REFERENCES

Bates, E. (1976). Pragmatics and sociolinguistics in child language. In D. Morehead and A. Morehead (Eds.), *Normal and deficient child language*. Baltimore: University Park Press.

Bellugi U. and Klima, E. (1972, June). The roots of language in the sign talk of the deaf. *Psychology Today*, pp. 61–76.

Black, J. (1971). Speech pathology for the deaf. In L. Connor (Ed.), *Speech for the deaf child: Knowledge and use*. Washington, DC: Alexander Graham Bell Association for the Deaf.

Bloom, L. (1970). *Language development: Form and function in emerging grammars*. Cambridge, MA: MIT Press.

Bloom, L. (1973). *One word at a time*. The Hague: Mouton.

Bloom, L. and Lahey, M. (1978). *Language development and language disorders*. New York: John Wiley & Sons.

Bowerman, M. (1979). The acquisition of complex sentences. In P. Fletcher and M. Garman (Eds.), *Language acquisition*. Cambridge: Cambridge University Press.

Brown, R. (1973). *A first language*. Cambridge, MA: Harvard University Press.

Brown, R., and Bellugi, U. (1964). Three processes in the child's acquisition of syntax. *Harvard Educational Review, 34,* 133–151.

Bruner, J. (1978). The role of dialogue in language acquisition. In A. Sinclair, R. Jarvella, and W. Levelt (Eds.), *The child's conception of language.* New York: Springer-Verlag.

Bruner, J. (1983). *Child's talk: Learning to use language.* New York: W. W. Norton.

Calvert, D. (1962). Speech sound duration and the surd-sonant error. *Volta Review, 64,* 401–402.

Cazden, C. (1972). *Child language and education.* New York: Holt, Rinehart and Winston.

Chomsky, N. (1957). *Syntactic structures.* The Hague: Mouton.

Clark, E. (1971). On the acquisition of the meaning of *before* and *after. Journal of Verbal Learning and Verbal Behavior, 10,* 266–275.

Clark, E. (1978). Awareness of language: Some evidence from what children say and do. In A. Sinclair, R. Jarvella, and W. Levelt (Eds.), *The child's conception of language.* New York: Springer-Verlag.

Cohen, D., Caparulo, B., and Wetstone, H. (1981). The emergence of meanings and intentions: Mothers' dialogue with normal and language-impaired children. *Psychiatric Clinics of North America, 4,* 489–508.

Cromer, R. (1976). The cognitive hypothesis of language acquisition and its implication for child language deficiency. In D. Morehead and A. Morehead (Eds.), *Normal and deficient child language.* Baltimore: University Park Press.

de Villiers, J. and de Villiers, P. (1978). *Language acquisition.* Cambridge, MA: Harvard University Press.

Edwards, M. (1974). Perception and production in child phonology: The testing of four hypotheses. *Journal of Child Language, 1,* 205–219.

Eimas, P. (1985, January). The perception of speech in early infancy. *Scientific American,* 46–52.

Ferguson, C. and Garnica, O. (1975). Theories of phonological development. In E. H. Lenneberg and E. Lenneberg (Eds.), *Foundations of language development: A multi-disciplinary approach* (Vol. 1). New York: Academic Press.

Fitzgerald, E. (1949). *Straight language for the deaf.* Washington, DC: The Alexander Graham Bell Association for the Deaf.

Fromkin, U., Krashen, S., Curtis, S., Rigler, D., and Rigler, M. (1978). The development of language in Genie: A case of language acquisition beyond the critical period. In M. Lahey (Ed.), *Readings in childhood language disorders.* New York: John Wiley & Sons.

Galenson, E., Kaplan, E., and Sherkow, S. (1983). The mother–child relationship and preverbal communication in the deaf child. In J. Call, E. Galenson, and R. Tyson (Eds.), *Frontiers of infant psychiatry.* New York: Basic Books.

Golden-Meadow, S., and Mylander, C. (1984). Gestural communication in deaf children: The effects and noneffects of parental input on early language development. *Monographs of the Society for Research in Child Development, 49*(3-4, Serial No. 207).

Hudgins, C., and Numbers, M. (1942). An investigation of intelligibility of the speech of the deaf. *Genetic Psychology Monographs, 25,* 289–392.

Ingram, D. (1979). Phonological patterns in the speech of young children.

In P. Fletcher and M. Garman (Eds.), *Language Acquisition*. Cambridge: Cambridge University Press.

Jakobson, R. (1968). *Child language, aphasia and phonological universals* (A. Keiler, Trans.). The Hague: Mouton.

Karmiloff-Smith, A. (1979). Language development after five. In P. Fletcher and M. Garman (Eds.), *Language acquisition*. Cambridge: Cambridge University Press.

Kretschmer, R. and Kretschmer, L. (1986). Language in perspective. In D. Luterman (ed.), *Deafness in perspective*. San Diego: College-Hill Press.

Lane, H. (1967). *The wild boy of Aveyron*. Cambridge, MA: Harvard University Press.

Levelt, W., Sinclair, A., and Jarvella, R. (1978). Causes and functions of linguistic awareness in language acquisition: Some introductory remarks. In A. Sinclair, R. Jarvella, and W. Levelt (Eds.), *The child's conception of language*. New York: Springer-Verlag.

Lewis, M. (1951). *Infant speech: A study of the beginnings of language*. New York: Humanities Press.

Lewis, M. (1963). *Language, thought, and personality in infancy-childhood*. London: Harrap.

McCormick, L. (1984). Review of normal language acquisition. In L. McCormick and R. Schiefelbusch (Eds.), *Early language intervention*. Columbus, OH: Merrill.

McNeill, D. (1970). *The acquisition of language*. New York: Harper and Row.

Menyuk, P. (1969). *Sentences children use*. Research Monograph No. 52. Cambridge, MA: MIT Press.

Moores, D. (1982). *Educating the deaf: Psychology, principles, and practices*. Boston: Houghton Mifflin.

Morse, P. (1974). Infant speech perception: A preliminary model and review of the literature. In R. Schiefelbusch and L. Lloyd (Eds.) *Language perspectives: Acquisition, retardation, and intervention*. Baltimore: University Park Press.

Nelson, K. (1974). Concept, word and sentence: Interrelations in acquisition and development. *Psychological Review, 481*, 267–285.

Newport, E., Gleitman, H., and Gleitman, L. (1977). Mother, I'd rather do it myself: Some effects and non-effects of maternal style. In C. Snow and C. Ferguson (Eds.), *Talking to children: Language input and acquisition*. New York: Cambridge University Press.

Phillips, J. (1973). Syntax and vocabulary of mother's speech to young children: Age and sex comparisons. *Child Development, 44*, 182–185.

Russell, W., Quigley, S., and Power, D. (1976). *Linguistics and deaf children*. Washington, DC: Alexander Graham Bell Association for the Deaf.

Schlesinger, H. and Meadow, D. *Sound and Sign: Childhood deafness and mental health*. Berkeley: University of California Press.

Simmons, A. (1965). Comparison of spoken and written language of deaf and hearing children at five age levels. *Report of the proceedings of the forty second meeting of the Convention of American Instructors of the Deaf*. Washington, DC: Government Printing Office.

Slobin, D. (1978). A case study of early language awareness. In A. Sinclair, J. Jarvella, and W. Levelt (Eds.), *The child's conception of language*. New York: Springer-Verlag.

Subtelny, J. (1977). Assessment of speech with implications for training. In F. Bess (ed.), *Childhood deafness: Causation, assessment, and management.* New York: Grune & Stratton.

Winitz, H. (1969). *Articulatory acquisition and behavior.* New York: Appleton-Century-Crofts.

CHAPTER 5

Parents Are Teachers

Parents, in general, do not consider themselves to be teachers. Teachers, as perceived by many parents, are professionals who have spent years studying and practicing their profession. Yet a child's education begins at birth, and if teaching is at all involved with the learning process, parents are teachers, and what is more important, they are the child's first teachers. Admittedly, the "parent teacher" arrives at this position amid different circumstances from the "professional teacher." The former has no minimum nor maximum age requirement, no experience prerequisites, no certification nor licensing requirements to fulfill, no citizenship qualifications to comply with.

Some parents, especially new parents, feel uncomfortable in their roles and seek advice and counsel from time to time. Formerly, middle-class parents more often than not consulted their pediatricians or family practice physicians for advice and guidance. More recently they have also purchased and devoured books concerning child development and desirable child rearing practices. In 1978, there were over 200 child care manuals in print (Clarke-Stewart, 1981).

If working-class and lower-income families took advantage of all the books and advice from the popular news media, such an act did not close the gap in school achievement between middle-class and lower-income children. The revelation in the 1960s of the deficits experienced by the latter group stimulated the tremendous thrust of federal support for programs that would help close the gap. Programs such as Head Start, the DARCEE program (Gilmer, Miller, and Gray, 1970), the Ypsilanti Perry Preschool Project (Weikart, Rogers, and Adcock, 1971), the Florida Parent Education Infant and Toddler Programs (Gordon, 1969), and the Parent Child Development Centers (PCDC) which were initiated in 1970 by the United States Office of Economic Opportunity (Andrews, Blumenthatl, Johnson, Kahn, Ferguson, Lasater, Malone, and Wallace, 1982) had as their goal the enhancement of development of children from low socioeconomic homes through helping parents become more effective child-rearing agents.

Bronfenbrenner's evaluation (1974) of many of the programs affirmed the value of the programs which had parental involvement components. Later studies have continued to confirm the fact that children's achievement and parental behavior can be influenced by parent education programs (Andrews et al., 1982; Beller, 1979; Clarke-Stewart and Apfel, 1978; Levenstein, 1977; Slaughter, 1983; Zigler and Berman, 1983). The programs cited in these studies were for the most part designed for children and parents (usually mothers) of low socioeconomic status. These were children with no sensory deficits who, along with their mothers, benefited from the guidance and assistance provided by the various programs. The mothers were helped to view themselves as teachers of their children, people who could make a difference in their children's success in school and later years (Bromwich, 1981). They were helped to see that they could control many aspects of their lives that they formerly had thought of as out of their control, and that their children had the potential to learn and achieve. Such aspirations had not previously been these mothers' viewpoints.

More recently, a program developed by the Early Childhood Education Section of the Missouri Department of Education (1982) has been initiated, which focuses on new parents as first teachers of their children. This program is based on the work of White (1980), and provides services to families from the third trimester of pregnancy until the children are three years of age. The formative findings have been most encouraging so far as the parents' acceptance of the program and the children's progress are concerned (White, 1985).

Many of the families discussed above have had grave problems which appear to have been somewhat alleviated by professional assistance. What of the families with a handicapped child? They, too, have most serious problems, problems sometimes compounded by low-income and low socioeconomic status. Moreover, many handicaps transcend all social, economic, and educational strata. No amount of social prestige, wealth, or education can compensate for the intrusion of a handicap on a "normal" family constellation.

PARENTS OF HANDICAPPED INFANTS

Professionals working with handicapped infants and children recognized the need for early intervention, even before such programs were widespread for nonhandicapped children from so-called disadvantaged environments. However, many of the early programs did not provide the services for parents that are now considered essential for any measurable (re)habilitation. Programs now have various formats and various objectives depending on the populations they serve, but practically all programs recognize and provide for the fact that both parents of a handicapped child suffer extreme emotional trauma when they are faced with the realization that they have a handicapped child (Bristol and Gallagher, 1980).

Parents usually anticipate the birth of a child with great joy and excitement. When this event is marred by the birth of a handicapped child, a flood of other emotions erupt. The stages and variety of these feelings have been described variously by a number of investigators (Benjamin, 1985; Moses, 1985; Osofsky and Connors, 1981; Project RHISE, 1980; Schlesinger and Meadow, 1972; Shearer and Shearer, 1977; Shontz, 1965; Simmons-Martin, 1976; Tulloch, 1983). A common thread appears in all of the accounts.

Stage 1

The first reaction to the initial diagnosis is shock. Parents have wished for and expected a "normal" child. Now their dreams are shattered, and they feel devastated and helpless. The shock has numbed them into a state of docility. They are unable to assimilate what information is given them, as they are not functioning in a normal manner. It has been reported that sometimes after learning the diagnosis for the first time, parents are utterly and literally lost, unable even to locate their cars in the parking lot.

Stage 2

After the initial shock, a number of emotions and feelings arise. Parents may appear to be bitter, anxious, or sad. They may be preoccupied with themselves. They may go through a period of introspection in which they are searching for the reason for their child's handicap. They are dealing with guilt, anger, and grief. They frequently vent their anger at the professionals, as they seek to pinpoint the blame.

Stage 3

At this stage, the parents are often in a state of panic. Moreover, they are confused, unable to plan, unable to understand the situation and still not ready to absorb what the professionals have to impart. In addition, they often are in a state of denial and may doubt the diagnosis. They are prone to seek other opinions, and in some cases, seek miracle cures. They may try to "bargain" with God and turn to religion; they may feel that they are being punished for some wrongdoing on their part; their anxiety may cause them to be hesitant to become attached to the child, for fear of deepening the pain. For some parents, children represent extensions of themselves, and the advent of a handicapped child impairs their self-image beyond restoration.

Stage 4

If the situation becomes overwhelming, it is natural to want to escape, so parents often retreat from the situation. Sometimes, this retreat is overt, sometimes it is subtle. They may seek custodial care for the child, or daily programs that will relieve them of the responsibility that they feel unable to assume. They may seem unable or unwilling to follow instructions, and may make no attempt to take part in the amelioration of the handicap. A more subtle form of escaping from the situation evidences itself when a parent keeps trying to put the baby to sleep, to remove him from the need of immediate care.

Stage 5

When parents are at last able to achieve realistic expectations and give appropriate help to their child, they accept the situation with great sorrow. They go through a period of grief not unlike the mourning one experiences for a deceased relative or friend. No doubt they are mourning the child who might have been. In strong family relationships, the parents experience an even stronger bond with each other, and are able to reorganize their lives and adjust emotionally.

Arrival at this stage does not mean that the adjustments parents of handicapped children must make are completed. On the contrary, as new crises surface, as new programs, new medical problems arise, parents will have to go through additional emotional adjustments. Like all parents, those of hearing-impaired children will experience rough times and have tough decisions to make, but the problem for these parents are exaggerated in their enormity and their consequences.

FAMILIES OF HEARING-IMPAIRED CHILDREN

The stages described in the preceding section may differ somewhat in their onset for parents of hearing-impaired children. For example, some handicaps (such as severe visual impairments, Down's syndrome, cerebral palsy, or spina bifida) may be apparent at the moment of birth. In contrast, hearing impairment more often than not is not apparent. Hearing-impaired babies can be as robust and healthy as hearing babies. Many parents' assumption that they have a perfectly normal infant is even, on occasion, confirmed by the pediatrician. Sensorineural hearing impairment is not discernible from a routine examination of the external and middle ear. Thus, the parents who have experienced no high-risk factors during the pregnancy and birth process and have no familial deafness can be totally unaware of what awaits them. Even high-risk factors, such as familial deafness, low birth weight, complications during pregnancy or childbirth, viral infections during pregnancy, low Apgar scores, high bilirubin levels (jaundice), and anoxia (low oxygen supply to the brain), do not always result in hearing impairments, or other handicapping conditions for that matter. Parents of babies who are at risk from one or more of these factors can still hope for a normal child.

It is understandable then, that parents of hearing-impaired children should question, "Why? Why me? Why my child?" perhaps even more so than parents of children with handicaps that are immediately observable. In many if not most cases, one parent or both have suspected a hearing impairment. Often they do not share their suspicions with each other in an effort to spare the partner what is hoped to be unnecessary anxiety. Nevertheless, when the diagnosis is confirmed, the parents experience shock, perhaps greater shock than that of the parents who faced the trauma of a handicapping condition when the baby was born and the main concern perhaps was for the child's survival.

Parents are individuals and do not progress through the described stages at the same rate or in a straight path. They progress and they regress individually. At the same time, they all have one thing in common: they are experiencing great pain. The stages of grief and pain are there, but vary from parent to parent in intensity and sequence. It is possible that some parents may not experience all the stages or pass through them so rapidly that they are not perceived by either the parent or the parent-infant facilitator, the professional who counsels with the parents on a regular basis.

In my experience, it appears that the parents of adopted children endure less stress and anxiety than natural parents. With the problem of guilt removed, the parents are more able to accept the handicap. There may also be racial and ethnic differences. Mexican-American parents, for instance, seem to accept the handicap as an act of God, something that

God has planned for them. Thus, it is their obligation to love and provide for the child in the best manner possible, which they are eager to do, and they gratefully accept professional assistance. These are generalizations, of course, and should not be construed as applicable to all parents in these categories.

Hearing-impaired parents of hearing-impaired children present a different situation also. Whereas many hearing-impaired parents hope their child will have normal hearing, they half expect that the child will be hearing-impaired. There is virtually no adjustment for the parents to make, and there is no delay in language stimulation for the infant. However, most hearing-impaired children are born to hearing parents (Rosen, 1986) who experience some or all of the emotions described above (Moses, 1985).

At the stage when they are denying the handicap, parents can be reaffirmed in their denial when the child demonstrates evidence of 'hearing." A very visually alert hearing-impaired infant can deceive an adult who wants to be deceived. Also, infants can respond to vibratory stimulation. Sometimes walking, even inaudibly, through a room will create enough vibration to awaken a sleeping infant, as any parent will attest. For a parent looking for signs of hearing, such incidents can easily qualify.

The parents are not the only members of the family constellation affected by the intrusion of a hearing-impaired child. Parents' child-rearing practices and attitudes toward the nonhandicapped children in the family can be dramatically altered with the advent of the handicapped child. The entire spectrum, from neglect to overindulgence, can occur while the parents are making adjustments to the trauma of bringing a handicapped child into the family, and even afterwards. Parents may spend an inordinate amount of time with the handicapped child, increasing the chance of serious sibling rivalry or neglect of the other children. In some cases, the hearing siblings are saddled with the responsibility of caretaker for the hearing-impaired family member. This situation can occur easily if the hearing-impaired child has an older sibling, but can occur even when the normally hearing sibling is younger (Landry and Mottier, 1977, reported in Zucman, 1982).

Grandparents also are members of the family to be considered. They can be influential in helping or hindering the adjustments made by the immediate family members. Parents of young children are usually young themselves and often still dependent on their parents for advice and approval and sometimes even financial assistance. Therefore, the grandparents' acceptance or rejection of any aspect of the hearing-impaired child's relationship to the parents, siblings, or even the professionals can be enhanced or diminished by their attitudes.

Families of handicapped children, nevertheless, are first of all families and as such have feelings similar to those of any family. Each family, including the parents, the siblings, the grandparents, and any substitute caregivers, has its own needs, hopes, desires, ambitions, expectations, and frustrations, as well as attitudes because of the handicap. Therefore, all families cannot be treated alike any more than all hearing-impaired children can be treated alike.

PARENTS LEARN TO TEACH

The parent–infant facilitator's student is the parent, not the child, but the student has to be ready to learn, and most parents of newly identified hearing-impaired children are not yet ready for direct instruction (Figure 5-1). The professional plays a very important role all the time, but it is especially important during the early stages. Faced with the positive

Figure 5-1. *A mother is labeling objects and events in the child's environment.*

evidence of an impairment from the medical and audiological evaluations, which often confirms the parents' own misgivings, the parents may express anger that is sometimes directed at the professional (Simmons-Martin 1976). The parent–infant facilitator must recognize this pattern and not react to the anger. By the time the parents are referred to the (re)habilitation program they may have been exposed to other professionals who have exacerbated their problems rather than mitigated them. Previous encounters may have been with a professional who presented the shocking facts with no explanations nor offers of help. Another may have painted such a dismal picture that the parents suffered even greater shock. Still another may have minimized the problem, distorting the true facts and giving the parents false expectations.

It is no wonder that some parents want to "shop around" for other opinions. In this instance, the parent–infant facilitator must refer the parents to reliable and appropriate professionals who will be direct, honest, yet warm and sympathetic. Where there are divergent management theories, parents should be so advised. They should have the options explained to them by the advocates of the various philosophies. Under no circumstances should they be pressured or hurried into making irrevocable decisions at this time when they are coping with so many problems. The role of the counselor here needs to be one of complete acceptance of the parents' dilemmas. The counselor needs to allow ample time for the parents to sift out their options and make choices that conform to their family structure, their financial and human resources, and their personalities.

An otologist of my acquaintance never told parents of a serious hearing impairment without immediately having the parents of an older hearing-impaired child, parents who had been through the trauma that the current parents are going through, get in touch with the new parents. He always chose parents who, along with their child, had made a good adjustment. In the early stages especially, opportunities for parents to talk to other parents can prove to be very helpful. Parents of older deaf children provide an excellent resource, enabling parents of young children to cope with their negative feelings.

It cannot be emphasized too strongly that each family must be considered unique, and all aspects of the family structure should influence the approach used for each family. Educated, middle-class parents who are accustomed to dealing with medical and educational professionals may not be intimidated during their encounters with the various professionals. In contrast, lower- and working-class families may be extremely uncomfortable with such professionals and very likely will not comprehend the jargon. They may not seek answers to questions that are bothering them for fear of appearing ignorant or for lack of enough understanding to pose the question. Even more serious is the problem of families who speak little or no English. To relate to these parents through an interpreter is very difficult. All families may need technical terms such as *decibel, Hertz, audiogram, sensorineural, conductive, threshold, tympanogram* explained to them later, when they are advanced enough in their adjustment to comprehend. However, during the initial stage, the parents are unable to retain much, if any, of the important information given them. The parent–infant facilitator should provide much repetition and should present the parents with a written account of the most important facts so that they can be referred to and discussed later (Simmons-Martin, 1976).

The infant is ready to learn, and does so, from the moment of birth (Anastasiow, 1979). He is able to become emotionally and physiologically involved immediately (Brazelton, 1981; Field, 1980; Stern, 1980). Moreover, the family structure appears to be "the most effective and economical system for fostering the development of the child" (Bronfenbrenner, 1974). Learning takes place gradually and naturally under ordinary conditions, but in the case of the hearing-impaired child the "family" or parents are not functioning as ordinary parents do; thus there is a hiatus in the learning process for the child. The trauma the parents are experiencing, as well as the child's hearing deficit, interrupt the flow of communication between the child and parents.

The consequence of the lack of communication is a serious deficit in the development of affect, a most important factor in the health and development of the infant (Greenstein, Greenstein, McConville, and Stellini, 1976). When that domain has been damaged by the discovery of the child's handicap, the bonding between parents and child is restricted. In order to help the parents adjust to the child's handicap, the counselor needs to be sensitive to the parents' feelings and be able to identify how far in the process of acceptance the family has advanced. Just listening to the parents and allowing them to share their feelings, both overt and covert, may be the most helpful thing the counselor can do at that time. It can reveal valuable information to the counselor, and it can help the parents verbalize their problems.

The parent–infant facilitator must resist the temptation to assume the teaching of the child, no matter how frustrating the lack of active parental input to the child is. The facilitator's time will be well spent as an interested listener who talks about children in general, not about the handicap. The facilitator should discuss the universal role of parenthood, and supplement these discussions with films, slides, or books which focus on good parenting skills. Even though the facilitator may have long been ready to initiate educational techniques, the parents may not have been, and a premature start might prove to be more harmful than helpful. This postponement is even more important among parents whose parenting skills may be deficient. The first order of importance is the development of positive affect, and this must be established before any (re)habilitation process can be established.

GOOD PARENTING–GOOD TEACHING

Only after the prerequisites of accepting the handicap and developing strong, positive affect have been accomplished can the parents begin to learn to be teachers. When we say that parents are teachers, we mean that they are natural teachers, not classroom teachers. We want them to learn the parenting skills that have proved to be successful with hearing children, so that they can emulate the practices (Figure 5-2). The emphasis here is on being a good parent, not on being a good teacher. A good parent is a good teacher naturally. Because our goal is for the hearing-impaired child to learn language as nearly as possible the way the hearing child does, we will want the parents of the hearing-impaired child to provide the same kind of stimulation that parents of hearing children do.

Unfortunately, many parents do not know nor understand the importance of the early stages of learning. Nor do they realize the the need for sensory stimulation. Most adults do not know the stages of child development. Some know intuitively what a child is capable of at certain ages, but they do not know what skills and knowledge are requisite for subsequent skills. More importantly, most do not understand the handicapping condition, or what measures will ameliorate its effects. Certainly, there are few who are aware of ways language is acquired and the adult's role in its acquisition. Contrary to the myth, "Mother knows best," many parents do not "know best," as evidenced by the studies and programs of the 1960s and 1970s mentioned earlier.

Figure 5-2. *Parents learn by observing classroom activities.*

White and Watts (1973) describe good parenting skills as not requiring "teaching" per se. On the contrary, in their study, mothers whose children were developing extremely well simply provided access to many objects and diverse situations. They served as a resource, both instrumental and emotional, and they consistently set limits, both physical and psychological. Moreover, they offered abundant linguistic input and stimulation from which their children could infer the grammar of the language. They provided ample opportunities for safe explorations, and they countered the young child's negativism with alternatives. The mothers of these very successful children did not feel that they were "teaching" their children; they had no specific schedules or plans. Instead, they incorporated these positive attributes into their daily lives. Some of the encounters with their children lasted only a minute or two. Some of the responses to requests for attention were only a few words assuring the child that he had been listened to and understood.

Parents need to learn that they do not need elaborate equipment or surroundings to provide a stimulating environment. Any household has an abundance of materials that are exciting to a young child. Beating a pan with a spoon can give as much satisfaction as an expensive drum; empty spools for thread strung together are as exciting as commercial wooden ones. The daily activities of the home, no matter what the socioeconomic level, contain all the teaching situations a parent needs to provide a stimulating environment. The essentials of a child's life—eating, sleeping, bathing, dressing, playing—are a curriculum in themselves. Parents who naturally and intuitively do not know how to exploit the natural situations can learn how, and it can be a joyful experience, not a burdensome chore. The joys of parenthood can be attained by parents of hearing-impaired children once the parents are ready to learn what they must do. The professional is obligated to show the way (Figure 5-3).

FATHERS ARE PARENTS TOO

The changing social and economic climate in the United States has attracted many mothers into the work force. Whether this movement or some other force has been the catalyst, fathers, too, are now being seen as caregivers of their children. They are often actively involved in the preparation for birth, and the birth process itself. The idea of middle-class fathers being present at the birth of their children was considered lunatic a generation ago. Recent research, however, has shown that fathers can be as involved and as sensitive to their infants as mothers (Parke and Tinsley, 1981). Other studies have demonstrated that mothers' and fathers' behaviors are different in the amount of time and type of interaction. The difference in amount of time decreases over time, however, and "fathers as well as mothers appear sensitive to the changing nature of the infant" (Belsky,

Gilstrap, and Rovine, 1984). Yet, since there are substantial differences in paternal and maternal interactions, it seems therefore very important for any child, but especially a handicapped child, to have both kinds of contact.

Fathers of infant and preschool handicapped children enrolled in programs were found to spend as much time with their children as fathers of normal infants (Linder and Chitwood, 1984). The fathers felt that both parents carried the responsibility for the education of their children, and that they wanted very much to be involved in the experience. Another interesting finding was that the most frequently reported "first choice" for describing their feelings was that they were coping with the situation fairly well now that their child was enrolled in a program. The study revealed also that fathers were eager to have options of services available to them. They responded favorably to such items as newsletters describing their child's progress, training programs in ways to work with their children, videotapes, films, and other resource materials.

In another study, Markowitz (1984) suggests ideas to involve fathers in programs to a greater extent. She suggests that program staffs should

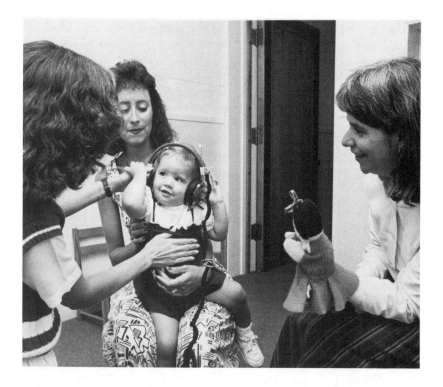

Figure 5-3. *The parent–infant facilitator and the educational audiologist work in tandem.*

be comfortable working with fathers, and *expect* fathers to be involved. This might mean that the program would have to provide flexible hours for fathers who cannot participate in sessions during traditional working hours. It is suggested further that programs make a concerted effort to seek male service providers. Another finding was that fathers are more likely to participate in one-to-one activities than group sessions.

There is now strong evidence that fathers are important to the development of young children, handicapped or not. Thus, it behooves programs providing services for handicapped infants and children to assure that fathers as well as mothers are among the teachers they produce.

SUMMARY

Parents are children's first teachers, even though most parents do not consider themselves as such. The natural "teaching" abilities of parents of handicapped children are often aborted due to the shock and trauma that they experience when their child's handicap is diagnosed. Parents of hearing-impaired children may experience even greater difficulties, since that handicap is usually not diagnosed at birth, and they can be misled at first into thinking that their infant is perfectly normal. Parents of all handicapped children go through many stages of adjustment before they are ready to accept instruction from professionals. Parents, with the help of professionals, can learn good parenting skills, but professionals must be careful to consider each family on an individual basis, as each family is unique and so are its needs and problems. Fathers, especially, are to be included as members of the (re)habilitation team, and most fathers are eager to be so considered.

REFERENCES

Anastasiow, N. (1979). Current issues in child development. In A. Simmons-Martin and D. Calvert (Eds.),*Parent–infant intervention: Communication disorders.* New York: Grune & Stratton.

Andrews, S., Blumenthal, J., Johnson, D., Kahn, A., Ferguson, C., Lasater, T., Malone, P., and Wallace, D. (1982). The skills of mothering: A study of parent child development centers. *Monographs of the Society for Research in Child Development. 47*(2, Serial No. 198).

Beller, E. (1979). Early intervention programs. In J. Osofsky (Ed.), *Handbook of infant development.* New York: John Wiley & Sons.

Beksky, J., Gilstrap, B., and Rovine, M. (1984). The Pennsylvania infant and family development project. I: Stability and change in mother–infant and father–infant interactions in a family setting at one, three, and nine months. *Child Development, 55*, 692–705.

Benjamin, B. (1985). *A special child in the family: A guide for parents.* San Marcos, TX: Southwest Texas State University.

Brazelton, T. (1981). *On becoming a family.* New York: Delacorte.

Bristol, M. and Gallagher, J. (1980). The changing role of parents of handicapped children. In C. Ramey and P. Trohanis (Eds.), *Finding and educating the high risk and handicapped infant.* Chapel Hill, NC: Technical Assistance Development System (TADS).

Bromwich, R. (1981). *Working with parents.* Baltimore: University Park Press.

Bronfenbrenner, U. (1974). *Is early intervention effective? A report on longitudinal evaluation of preschool programs* (Vol. 2). Washington, DC: Department of Health, Education, and Welfare.

Clarke-Stewart, K. (1981). Parent education in the 1970s. *Educational Evaluation and Policy Analysis, 3,* 47–58.

Clarke-Stewart, K., and Apfel, N. (1978). Evaluating parent effects on child development. In L. Shulman (Ed.), *Review of research in education* (Vol. 6). Itaska, IL: F. F. Peacock.

Field, T. (1980). Interactions of high-risk infants: Quantitative and qualitative differences. In D. Sawin, R. Hawkins, L. Walker, J. Penticuff (Eds.), *Psychological risks in infant environment transactions.* New York: Brunner/Mazel.

Gilmer, B., Miller, J., and Gray, S. (1970). *Intervention with mothers and young children: A study of intra-family effects.* (DARCEE Papers and Reports, 4, No. 1.) Nashville, TN: George Peabody College for Teachers.

Gordon, I. (1969). *Early childhood stimulation through parent education* (Final report). Gainsville, FL: Institute for the Development of Human Resources, University of Florida. (ERIC Document Reproduction Service No. 138 166)

Greenstein, J., Greenstein, B., McConville, K., and Stellini, L. (1976). *Mother–infant communication and language acquisition in deaf infants.* New York: Lexington School for the Deaf.

Levenstein, P. (1977). The mother–child home program. In M. Day and R. Parker (Eds.), *The preschool in action* (2nd ed.). Boston: Allyn and Bacon.

Linder, T. and Chitwood, D. (1984). The needs of fathers of young handicapped children. *Journal of the Division for Early Childhood, 8,* 133–139.

Markowitz, J. (1984). Participation of fathers in early chldhood special education programs: An exploratory study. *Journal of the Division for Early Childhood, 8,* 119–131.

Missouri Department of Elementary and Secondary Education. (1982). *Parents as first teachers.* Jefferson City, MO: Author.

Moses, K. (1985). Infant deafness and parental grief: Psychosocial early intervention. In F. Powell, T. Finitzo-Hieber, S. Friel-Patti, and D. Henderson (Eds.), *Education of the hearing impaired child.* San Diego: College-Hill Press.

Osofsky, J., and Connors, K. (1981). Mother–infant interaction: An integrative view of a complex system. In J. Osofsky (Ed.), *Understanding and working with parents of children with special needs.* New York: Holt, Rinehart and Winston.

Park, R. and Tinsley, B. (1981). The father's role in infancy: Determinants in caregiving and play. In M. Lamb (Ed.), *The role of the father in child development* (2nd ed.). New York: John Wiley & Sons.

Project RHISE. (1980). Outreach-Children's Development Center. Unpublished abstract of program. Rockford, IL.

Rosen, R. (1986). Deafness: A social perspective. In D. Luterman (Ed.), *Deafness in perspective*. San Diego: College-Hill Press.

Schlesinger, H., and Meadows, K. (1976). Emotional support for parents. In D. Lillie, P. Trohanis, and K. Goin (Eds.), *Teaching parents to teach*. New York: Walker.

Shearer, M. and Shearer, D. (1977). Parent involvement. In J. Jordan, H. Hayden, M. Karnes, and M. Woods (Eds.), *Early childhood education for exceptional children: A handbook of ideas and exemplary practices*. Reston, VA: Council for Exceptional Children.

Shontz, F. (1965). Reactions to crisis. *Volta Review, 67,* 364–370.

Simmons-Martin, A. (1976). A demonstration home approach with hearing-impaired children. In E. Webster (Ed.), *Professionals approach parents of handicapped children*. Springfield, IL: Charles Thomas.

Slaughter, D. (1983). Early intervention and its effects on maternal and child development. *Monographs of the Society for Research in Child Development. 48(4, Serial No. 202).*

Stern, D. (1980). Infant signals of readiness to communicate. In A. Reilly (Ed.), *The communication game*. New York: Johnson & Johnson Pediatric Round Table Series, No. 4.

Tulloch, D. (1983) Why me? Parental reaction to the birth of an exceptional child. *Journal of the Division for Early Childhood, 7,* 54–60.

Weikart, D., Rogers, L., and Adcock, C. (1971). *The cognitively oriented curriculum*. Urbana, IL: University of Illinois Press.

White, B. (1980). *A parent's guide to the first three years*. Englewood Cliffs, NJ: Prentice-Hall.

White, B. (1985, October). Missouri's new parents as teachers project. *Newsletter*. Newton, MA: The Center for Parent Education, 1.

White, B., and Watts, J. (1973). *Experience and environment*. Englewood Cliffs, NJ: Prentice-Hall.

Zigler, E., and Berman, W. (1983). Discerning the future of early childhood intervention. *American Psychologist. 38,* 894–906.

Zucman, E. (1982). *Childhood disability in the family*. New York: World Rehabilitation Fund.

CHAPTER 6

Parent–Infant Programs

The importance of the early years in learning of all kinds has been
well documented. For language, the early years are even more
important; some researchers say even critical. Although the concept of
a critical period for language acquisition has both its advocates and critics,
it cannot be denied that children in all cultures learn their language, at
a very young age, and become quite proficient in its use in a short period
of time. Educators of hearing-impaired children with long experience will
attest to the fact that children who enter programs at a "late" age (six years
or so) do not learn language as easily as children who, along with their
parents, have been involved in a (re)habilitation program at earlier ages.

The basic approach in a parent–infant program is to help the parents,
especially the mother, with the young hearing-impaired child in the home.
The home, the total family constellation, shapes the child's total
development— physical, cognitive, social, and particularly linguistic—
through experiences it provides (Simmons-Martin, 1981). It is not by
accident that one's native language is called the "mother tongue." It might
more appropriately be called the "family tongue." Involving the parents
and family is the major means of helping the hearing-impaired child.

RATIONALE FOR PARENT–INFANT PROGRAMS

Since the family is the most powerful educational delivery system in
the life of any child, and particularly a hearing-impaired child, family

involvement is imperative. Certain assumptions, therefore, underlie the parent–infant program rationale. They are:

1. There is an ideal, if not critical, time for intellectual growth and language learning (Bloom, 1964; McNeill, 1970). Psychologists increasingly believe that the experiences in early life affect intellectual growth and language acquisiton. Hence, the hearing-impaired child must be assured of having the rich experiences necessary for development.

2. The hearing-impaired child, like his normally hearing siblings, is genetically endowed to learn a language (Chomsky, 1980), and like them, needs language stimulation. The child needs to experience the *function* of language, and to observe the *content* as it is matched to experiences. Parents need to be shown ways to adapt to the child's deficiencies, while at the same time providing the appropriate and necessary quantity of input.

3. All sense perception needs to be trained. In addition to learning to use to their fullest capacities—the abilities to look, not just to see, to feel, not just to touch—the hearing-impaired child must learn to listen, not just to hear. He must learn to hear and respond to auditory signals, the most salient aspect of spoken language. These signals should be transmitted over proper amplification in order to become meaningful to the child.

4. Language acquisition is dependent upon adults who positively encourage the child to talk, to label his world, and to respond to the speech of others.

5. Spoken language skills improve with auditory feedback. Since the deficit with these children is such that it restricts the range of auditory perception, special attention needs to be directed to helping the child develop speech skills through listening, with the support of vision only when necessary.

6. Learning spoken communication proceeds in an orderly fashion, and parents need to reinforce the child's efforts at each stage. As is the case with a normally hearing child, the hearing-impaired one needs a speech climate to be provided. Beginning with vocalizations that eventually get shaped into meaningful speech, a child learns function, content, and form, (in that order) from parents and other family members. This sequence must occur likewise for the hearing-impaired child.

7. The early experiences that infants and young children encounter exert a powerful influence on their development (Kagan, Kearsley, and, Zelazo, 1980). Certain intellectual and emotional processes are particularly vulnerable to disturbance during the early months. These include sensory perception, language development, creative and abstract thinking, the ability to establish deep and meaningful interpersonal relationships, and the ability to control impulse in the interest of long-range goals (Schlesinger, 1985).

STRUCTURE

If intervention is to take place as early as possible in life, the setting for language learning should be the home; infants do not attend classes. For the infant in the sensorimotor period, the home is the wide, wide world. The personnel for this educational process is the parents or the principal caregiver. In other words, the "when" is as early as possible; the "where" is at home; and the "who" is the parents or surrogate (Figure 6-1).

The "how" of the program, whether the program is center-based or home-based or a combination, should be determined by the constraints of the agency providing the service and the special characteristics of the population being served. If families have no available transportation, a home-based program is called for. If the families are the kind who feel that having a professional enter their homes on a regular basis is an intrusion on their privacy, a center-based program would be more appropriate. The important issue is that entire families need to be served in a systematic and individual fashion. The serving program should either provide or have

Figure 6-1. *Early identification and repeated evaluations are important factors in (re)habilitation.*

access to complete medical, audiological, educational, and guidance services. Ordinarily all these services will not be available by a single agency, but the primary service provider should have contacts with the other agencies or personnel so that it can act as the clearing house to coordinate all the services being provided for any particular family.

LONG-RANGE PROGRAM GOALS

The long-range goal of any parent–infant program is the maximum exploitation of the child's innate abilities. This goal can be reached if parents are assisted in providing a stimulating home environment which promotes total growth in their child, if parents are helped to develop a warm, affectionate relationship with their child, if they are helped in setting and resetting realistic targets for achievement by their child, and if the total family can develop an accepting, not patronizing, attitude toward the child's handicap, so that the child can be just another member of the family who happens to have some special needs.

Most families cannot achieve these goals without professional help. Therefore, the professionals of the parent–infant program should have as their objectives the ability to:

1. Listen to the parents.
2. Deal with the parent(s)' feelings of shock, anger, denial, retreat, and grief by providing emotional support.
3. Determine the extent of the parents' background knowledge.
4. Provide information to the parents in a way that they can understand.
5. Help the parents become thoroughly familiar with the facts and implications of their child's problems as they become known.
6. Help the parents acquire confidence in their ability to cope effectively with the day-to-day problems of a handicapped child.
7. Assist the parents to achieve consistently firm but affectionate handling of the child in a variety of situations.
8. Help the parents establish a positive and warm affective interactive bonding with their infant by strengthening the positive aspects of parent–child interaction.
9. Help the parents provide a language environment which will promote language acquisition, taking into account the child's impaired sensitivity.
10. Help the parents learn to be sensitive to natural and informal situations in everyday life which make language more meaningful to the child, and to exploit these situations.

11. Teach parents to be alert to ideal opportunities not only for the development of communication skills but also the total, integrated development of the child.

12. Provide parents with information about available resources.

These objectives can be achieved only if the philosophy of the program is such that it considers each family as unique, with individual problems that require individual resolutions.

THE ROLE OF THE PARENT–INFANT FACILITATOR

The parent–infant facilitator's first objective is to help the parents pass through the negative emotional stages that the presence of a handicapped child can impose on them. At this time, the most effective strategy is to be a good listener. Just listening to the parents with empathy and patience may be the wisest expenditure of time. If the parents are ready for any input at all from the professional during this period when the parents are not yet ready to discuss the handicap directly, it might be a productive technique to discuss the universal parental role. The emphasis should be placed on skills for parenting of all children, rather than on the special needs of their handicapped child. If the handicapped child is a first-born, it is very likely that the parents are experiencing some problems that all new parents face, and they will probably appreciate advice on matters such as sleeping patterns, eating schedules, and other infant activities. The facilitator may have to work more to improve the parenting skills than to get the (re)habilitation process established.

Often, the mother and father are not at the same stage of acceptance and are not experiencing the same feelings simultaneously. The parent–infant facilitator must be sensitive to such a situation and be able to assess the progress of each parent. In this case, the main priority should be given to helping the parents adjust to their child's handicap and to facilitating the flow of communication between the parents. The parents cannot transmit positive affect to their child if they are having difficulty communicating with each other. Again, patient listening is the best, but not the easiest, strategy. The professional is eager to initiate the program, and regrets every day that it must be delayed.

The professional must be particularly sensitive to subtle signals that the parents have not yet accepted the handicapping condition, so as not to be misled by outward signs into thinking the parents are ready to embark on a (re)habilitation program. For example, one father would not give permission to have his child included in a television presentation, because he did not want the child exposed to the whole city as a handicapped child.

This parent was still struggling with his feelings of guilt, inadequacy, or grief. He could not admit the handicap to himself; how could he tell it to the whole world? There are many covert signals to which the professional must be alert: frequent canceling of appointments; strong disagreements with the professional; expecting excessively long sleeping periods of the baby; seeking custodial care for the child, so as to avoid the care-giving tasks; these among other avoidance tactics.

The professional must be sure that the parents know that such feelings are normal and that they, the parents, are not lacking in parental love nor emotional strength. In general, a direct approach is not the strategy to use. If parents cannot recognize their feelings themselves, they will not appreciate being told that they have not accepted their child's handicap. Often, though, a parent can dispel negative feelings just by talking about them, and the professional's role is to be a good listener. By doing so, the professional helps the parents sort out and analyze their feelings. The professional should never tell parents she knows how they feel unless she herself is a parent of a hearing-impaired child.

Once the parents have come to grips with their situation and the fact that they are the most powerful forces in their child's development, the (re)habilitation can begin. The emphasis now is to help the parents be first rate parents, not second rate teachers. There now is great stress on *process*, not curriculum. The range of experiences, as well as the variety of situations presented by the child and the parents, require that the parent–infant facilitator assume a variety of roles. These roles include being:

1. A *listener*, because parents may have no one else with whom they can discuss their concerns about their child.
2. A *model*, who demonstrates activities and interaction with the child for the parents to imitate.
3. A *reinforcer*, who supports everything positive that the parent does.
4. A *reality tester*, who helps the parents test the reality of situations concerning themselves or their child.
5. An *activity director*, who gives ideas to the parents who are unsure of what to do.
6. An *interpreter*, who puts professional jargon into language that the parents can understand.
7. A *resource person*, who keeps abreast of the latest knowledge in child development, hearing impairment, hearing aids, medical advances (such as cochlear implants), legislation concerning handicapped individuals, and any other topic related to any particular child.
8. A *teacher*, who communicates rationale and objectives to the parents.
9. An *advocate*, for parents of handicapped children.

QUALIFICATIONS OF THE PARENT-INFANT
FACILITATOR

In addition to the roles which the parent–infant facilitator may be asked to serve, there are various requisite qualifications, both innate and acquired, that the professional must possess. Among the innate qualifications are:

1. Maturity, without personality deviations which might limit effectiveness.
2. Credibility within the community and, if possible, membership in the parents' culture.
3. A familiarity with the customs, values, and mores of the community served.
4. Fluency in the language of the community.
5. Respect for the individuals she serves, including the ability to maintain complete confidentiality of all information.
6. Adaptability, including being able to function in a variety of settings and with a variety of professionals.

Among the acquired characteristics the professional must possess are knowledge and skills including:

1. The fundamentals of child development including
   a. sensory and motor development
   b. social, emotional, and personality development
   c. language acquisition of normally developing children
   d. cognitive and perceptual development
   e. creativity in children.
2. Hearing and the implications of hearing impairments and auditory imperceptions on
   a. language acquisition, cognition, and adaptive behaviors
   b. language acquisition in pre- and post- lingually acquired impairment.
3. The nature of hearing impairments and their medical remediations, if any.
4. The basic concepts of the speech and hearing mechanisms and their functions.
5. Hearing aids, their capabilities and limitations.
6. Environmental influences on social, linguistic, and cognitive development.
7. Listening and interrelating skills and techniques.
8. Behavior modification techniques.
9. Competency in setting realistic objectives, the means of achieving them, and techniques for evaluating outcomes.

10. The ability to communicate with the deaf of the community (for example, deaf adults, deaf parents) and to be accepted by them.
11. The ability to handle group discussions and use creditable counseling techniques.
12. Cognizance of the roles of health, social, and religious agencies, and the ability to obtain assistance when needed (Grant, 1972).

The parent–infant facilitator has an added obligation when working with parents of a different culture. The facilitator must be careful not to impose values on the family, or imply in any manner that the family's culture is deficient in any way. The problem is more complicated when the family speaks a different language. Ideally, the professional would be from the same culture and be a native speaker, but when this is not possible, she certainly must develop sensitivities and knowledge of the family's structure and customs. If the facilitator has to work with the parents through an interpreter, the task will be even more difficult.

THE INDIVIDUAL CONFERENCE

Parent–infant programs vary in their structure and curricula, but all include individual parent conferences in which the professional counsels with the parents concerning their child (Figure 6-2). One of the basic characteristics of the individual conference is its inherent flexibility in terms of time and content. In general, the parent(s) and parent–infant facilitator meet weekly, but this certainly is not a fixed rule. It might be profitable to schedule a meeting after an audiologic or psychological evaluation so that the findings could be discussed and perhaps elucidated. The content can be very specific or not, but it is always highly confidential. The language of the professional will be geared to the intellectual and linguistic level of the individual parent(s). The intervener may even demonstrate with the child a procedure or activity for the parent, in order to clarify the significance of a principle. There are no set rules for the content or the format of the individual conference, but some guidelines for the parent–infant facilitator are in order:

1. Make the parent feel comfortable and accepted.
2. Be as patient with the parent as she expects the parent to be with the child.
3. Be genuinely interested in the parent(s) and meet their individual needs.
4. Be friendly yet objective, thereby avoiding too close personal relations.
5. Refrain from making moral judgments, showing surprise, disgust, or rejection.

Figure 6-2. *The parent–infant facilitator counsels with the parent(s) concerning the child.*

6. Focus only on the (re)habilitation of the child, and the parent's role as the child's real teacher.
7. Avoid letting the sessions become psychotherapy. If the parents need this kind of help, refer them to a mental health professional.
8. Delineate thoroughly, and positively reinforce, the activities that the parent(s) are carrying out successfully.
9. Summarize each session for the parent(s) so that they can experience success at what has been accomplished.
10. Help the parent(s) assess their progress and select their next objectives.
11. Keep written records of each session and record them as soon as possible after each session.

It is important to remember that the parent(s) are the students in this situation, and the professional is an observer. If the conference takes place in the child's home, a natural setting is provided. If the conference takes place in a center, as home-like an atmosphere as possible is most desirable. Many center programs have simulated or even actual "homes." The home should have areas that represent a kitchen, a living room, a bathroom, a bedroom, an outside yard. Actual rooms are better yet, but such elaborate arrangements are not always possible. Ideally, there will be appliances that really work, a refrigerator well stocked, as well as cupboards and cabinets that contain the usual contents.

The most desirable arrangement is for the entire family, the child, the parents, the grandparents, the siblings, even the babysitter, all to enter this setting for a (usually) weekly conference with the intervener, who is a teacher of the hearing-impaired and has had additional training in counseling parents of hearing-impaired infants. The mother or principal caregiver typically engages the child in some activity normal to the household routine, if at home, or a comparable activity, if at a center. During this session, the intervener attempts to help the parent seize every opportunity for language input. The adult demonstrates how well she is progressing, while the intervener comments appropriately.

Obviously, the parent–infant facilitator must be skilled in creating an atmosphere of ease, transforming apprehensions into creative energy, and helping the parents feel the need for interaction with their child. One of the main objectives of this conference is for the parents to realize that in every activity there is appropriate language for what the child is experiencing at that very moment. During a parent conference, the professional should never assume that because the parents nod their heads in apparent assent, that they have attained complete understanding. Genuine change is a time-dependent phenomenon and requires continuous exposure to reality based situations. Parents must be encouraged to be natural and as relaxed as possible.

STRATEGIES

Videotapes

The intervention curriculum is a *process* whereby the parent–infant facilitator attempts to modify the naturally occurring dynamics of the hearing-impaired child's home and family interaction to the child's advantage. Sometimes parents benefit most from specific instruction; sometimes they may require models; at other times they may want set experiences to imitate. In all instances, however, videotapes can be a very useful tool in leading them to develop their own unique strategies and skills. Parents can be videotaped in their homes or the center at regular (usually monthly) intervals. Immediately following the taping, the mother (or caregiver) views the filmed sequence and evaluates herself. In this way, she becomes aware of her strengths and abilities as well as her weaknesses. She and the professional then can discuss meaningfully the interaction between child and parent. Self-criticism is of much greater impact than subjective evaluation by the intervener, and the taped experience can be played and replayed to extract the maximum benefit from the session. As a result of viewing themselves, parents improve their existing "teaching" strategies and develop new ones. Experience has shown that skill at parenting seems to be more greatly enhanced through this type of evaluation than through the traditional didactic method.

Another benefit of videotaping is its value in recording progress. Parents can observe where they have been and how they have progressed over time. Most parents experience important positive reinforcement when they observe their progress. Also, the tapes serve as a basis for conferences when other family members who were not present at the taping are involved. When parents can monitor their interaction style, they usually can correct themselves, and generalize to their nonmonitored behavior the principles and strategies encouraged by the center.

Modeling

Another useful strategy in helping parents is modeling interaction behaviors for them. As mentioned previously, some parents need to have activities actually demonstrated for them. It may be necessary for the parent–infant facilitator to identify important techniques, such as producing an appropriate remark every time the child looks at the adult, or expanding the child's incomplete utterances. The teacher who models various skills must be certain that the parent demonstrates the exampled strategy during the conference to ensure that the parent is comfortable with the procedure. The parent–infant facilitator may feel it is necessary to demonstrate, rather than simply describe, other important techniques, such as always talking to the child at eye level. To do this requires that the adult either sit on the floor, kneel, or stoop to be at a comfortable eye level for the child. An alternative is to put the child on a counter or table or other raised surface, if that serves the purpose better.

The parent may have to have demonstrated how to get the child's attention without constantly using tactile means, but instead to stimulate him auditorially by calling his name or saying something such as "Look what I have!" Caution should be taken not to distract the child from an activity in which he is intensely interested; instead, use that activity for linguistic input.

Reinforcement

The parent–infant facilitator may find it necessary to model reinforcement techniques for the parent. It is very important that every vocalization that the child utters be reinforced immediately and positively. Vocalization is not the only behavior that should be reinforced, however; there are many others. Every time the child responds to any auditory stimulus, complies with the parent's or teacher's wishes, initiates an activity, or demonstrates curiosity about the environment or artifacts in it, the child should be strongly and positively reinforced. Parents need to learn to be alert to any action that could be commended.

In addition to alerting the parents to the need for positive reinforcement, the professional should see to it that all members of the family know the value of reinforcement. Every member should reinforce the actions of the hearing-impaired child. In addition, the one who reinforces the handicapped child should be praised too. The mother may have to be reminded to commend the hearing siblings when they reinforce or help in any way the hearing-impaired child.

Two more important aspects of reinforcement are that it must be consistent and that it should become nonconcrete as soon as possible. In other words, the child should be reinforced for every vocalization, but the degree of reinforcement should decrease with time: where a raisin or piece of cereal had been necessary at first, the reinforcers should, as soon as possible, be reduced to a smile or a pat on the head or a verbal compliment.

Interpretation

Another strategy that the parent–infant facilitator may need to employ is that of interpreting the child's action or intention to the parent. A normally hearing parent or a new parent may not be accustomed to the nonverbal communication of young children, and especially young hearing-impaired children. The parent may have to be alerted to a child's attempts at communication so that the action can be reinforced and be labeled linguistically.

Imitation

Still another useful strategy is that of imitating the verbal output of the child, no matter how primitive. After imitating the child's utterance, the parent should be shown how to expand or correct the utterance and have the child imitate the expanded version as nearly as possible (Simmons-Martin, 1978).

GROUP EDUCATION

Fundamental to the parents' understanding of the handicapping condition is their knowledge of the handicap. A program for parent groups is considered to be an essential part of a parent–infant program. During these sessions, there can be discussions of subjects such as language development, hearing aids, behavior modification, genetics, the hearing mechanism, and cochlear implants, to mention only a few subjects.

Presenters might be psychologists, pediatricians, adult hearing-impaired individuals, parents of older hearing-impaired children, educators of hearing as well as hearing-impaired children. The parents should set the objectives of these parent education groups. A wise policy is for the parents themselves to decide what the topics should be and do all the planning, including arranging for the speaker, the babysitters, the meeting time and place, and the honorarium, if appropriate.

Experience has shown that generally parents want, first of all, up-to-date and accurate scientific information regarding their children's handicap in language that they can understand. They want to know what effects the disability may have on the usual chart of child development, the emotional aspects of the handicap, and the way the handicap may affect their children's personalities and behavior. They want very pragmatic information on what they can do to help their children develop to their capacity, and what the parents may expect this capacity to be. In other words, they want to know what they have to look forward to. Obviously, all these questions cannot be answered by the professional, especially during the early stages of the (re)habilitation. Such predictions cannot be accurately made about very young normally hearing children, but parents seem not to be as anxious about these offspring.

These are the questions they often bring with a very strong sense of urgency to professional personnel at first. It is only later that they reveal that they need to know more about themselves, about their own special level of tolerance of the demands that are put on them. They need to have help in recognizing both where they are weak and where they are strong so that they can turn to appropriate services for help when such services are needed. It is at this later time that they want to know the effect of a handicapped child on the family as a whole, the strain this places on the marriage, the effect on siblings as they are growing up. It is obvious that the answers to these queries need to be individualized, and no one answer will be applicable to all families.

Some of the information parents need can be made available to them through printed material and in lectures to large groups. Yet the professional must be reminded that the "formal presentations" have their limitations, that parents will take from such readings and presentations only as much as they are able to absorb, and that they may react to some of the material in ways that no one can predict in advance.

In order to provide an atmosphere where parents can truly ventilate their feelings, there should be some meetings at which there are no teacher–counselors, audiologists, or other professionals closely related to the program services. In such a setting, parents will discuss matters with other parents, situations that they may be reluctant to discuss with a professional. The support they receive from each other can be as valuable as the professional advice and support they receive.

The (re)habilitation program needs to provide a variety of group experiences in order to address the needs of parents at the various stages of their adjustment. Some meetings could be for small groups of parents, perhaps only mothers whose children have been newly identified and enrolled in the program. Another could be for "continuing" mothers, and still a third could be a combination of groups (Figure 6-3). There should be sessions planned for fathers, both alone and with their wives. The importance of their participation in the total rehabilitation process cannot be overestimated.

ACTIVITIES

Because the greatest promoter of language is experience, we want the lives of the children to be full of rich experiences. In addition, we want to provide experiences abounding in basic cognitive and sensory stimulation, because early language development parallels growth in cognitive and other developmental domains. These experiences have verbal labels associated with them, which in turn assist in the storage of the language appropriate to them. By means of perception the child develops the intrinsic concepts and vocabulary connected to the experiences that have features in common. The child in this way receives the data by which

Figure 6-3. *Some parent meetings should be for small groups of parents.*

to infer the rules of the language to be learned. For example, "washing" is a concept which has a variety of possible linguistic forms—wash hands, wash face, wash hair, wash someone else's face and hands, wash dishes, wash pots, pans, and silver, wash clothes, wash the car, wash the dog, wash the windows, wash the floor, and on and on. Even though the implements use are varied—soap, sponge, washcloth, mop, machine, hose—there are features in common—water, soap, and some sort of rubbing action. However, the most important feature they all have in common is the symbol or word, *wash*. The ability to generalize the meaning of *wash* from one experience to another, and eventually to apply such meanings to abstract usage, is enhanced to a much greater extent when the word is experienced in a variety of settings, rather than even experiencing it many times in only one situation.

The appropriateness of the activity selected is part of the parent–infant facilitator's concern. Each family must be known well enough that the facilitator can guide the selection of activities in ways that will be beneficial. The choice of activity should be discussed with the mother prior to her demonstrating with her child the project she has planned for that visit. Many factors must be considered when planning experiences: the financial resources of the family; what the home is like; what siblings who may be present; the interests of the parent; the "usefulness" of the experience. Elaborate experiences requiring expensive toys or props are not necessary. The simpler the home environment, the simpler the experiences should be. This does not mean that simple homes and simple experiences are inferior in any way. The point is that any activity in any home can provide a rich linguistic experience.

AUDITORY ACTIVITIES

Paramount to environmental management is the shaping of auditory skills, for speech perception and speech production are reciprocal skills, each enhancing the development of the other (Ling, 1976). As soon as possible, before or immediately after enrollment in a (re)habilitation program, the child should be provided with hearing aids, with the objective that he will wear them consistently. Listening then becomes a crucial point of the early training, with the aim that it will become a part of the child's system of sensory intake. This result will not come about without some special emphasis on listening skills, and parents very likely will need guidance and practice in developing these skills.

At all times, parents need to be alert to maximizing the use of amplified sound. Of greatest significance is the speech of the parents and the child's auditory feedback of his own vocalizations. Parents should be instructed to talk to the child, but not aimlessly or indiscriminately. Rather, they need to talk about *the child's* interests, what *the child* is attending to, and what *the child* likes. Not only is the child ego-centered at this age, but he is still concretely oriented, which means that the content of the talking the parents do must be of the "here and now" variety. In listening to language, the child must associate speech with things important to him, delivered by people important to him.

Thus, an important activity that takes place during the individual conference is an "auditory" activity. The parents need to demonstrate, or have demonstrated to them if necessary, the auditory skills appropriate for their child at the various stages of progress. The parent–infant facilitator must be sure that the parent is cognizant of the hierarchy of listening skills that are requisite to auditory language comprehension and expressive language, the ultimate goals. Although parents are not expected to engage in formal auditory training sessions with very young children, they should be aware of the levels of auditory responses that lead to auditory language comprehension. The stages of detection, discrimination, and identification must precede comprehension (Erber, 1982).

At the early level of detection, the parents must be reminded that all activites must be fun for both the parents and child. Just as the hearing child gets pleasure from the cooing and gurgling sounds that adults use, the hearing-impaired child also should experience fun with sounds. Depending upon the child's hearing level, more or less time will be required to bring the child's attention to these sounds. If the child cannot hear or does not respond to speech sounds at first, parents should not despair, but instead target their efforts on more gross sounds. Environmental sounds may not lead directly to speech discrimination; nevertheless, they are important. It is important for the infant to know when the dog is barking, when the telephone is ringing, when a car comes into the driveway, when the dishwasher, washing machine, vacuum sweeper, or other appliances are operating. One advantage to listening to such gross sounds as these is that many of them create strong vibrations which can help alert the child to the acoustic event.

The transition of attention from gross environmental sounds to voice sounds can be an opportunity for the parents to become creative with their voices. The sounds they produce do not necessarily have to be speech sounds. They may imitate the child's squeaky and mechanical toys, or noises made by the household pets. They can assist the child at this identification stage by asking for identification of their imitations. They should sing songs for the child to identify. Songs are a fine activity because the child can feel the vibrations of the parent's voice if held close to the chest. The parent need to be alert to the child's increasing ability to identify gross and environmental sounds, and to proceed to speech sounds when the child is ready. They can promote the transition from the perception of gross sounds to vocal sounds by imitating any sounds that the child makes, making sure that the imitations are seen, felt, and heard (Simmons-Martin, 1975).

From this point on, the parents should be helped to develop the concepts that will lead to comprehension of auditory receptive language. Some of the strategies the parent may be expected to use are:

1. Talking about things that are interesting to the child, "tuning in" to him.
2. Talking about what the child is perceiving—seeing, feeling, tasting, smelling, doing—at the moment. These are the actions that need verbal labels.
3. Labeling verbally the child's playthings, food, clothing, body parts, as well as actions. The emphasis here is on the child's perceptual zone of the here and now.
4. Using complete but short sentences or phrases, and single words only as a last resort, for labeling.
5. Providing repetition of experiences with accompanying appropriate language. Children enjoy repeating pleasant experiences, and some concepts require repeated exposure before they are assimilated.
6. Expecting responses to verbal language, and showing pleasure in the child's responding and understanding.
7. Waiting for responses to verbal stimuli. It takes more time for hearing-impaired children to process auditory stimuli than it does normally hearing children.
8. Reinforcing all the child's efforts in a most positive fashion. (Simmons-Martin, 1976).

Expressive language cannot be anticipated until a corpus of receptive language is accumulated. The parents may need to demonstrate or have demonstrated to them some strategies concerning the fostering of expressive language, such as:

1. Listening and responding to the child. As stated earlier, every vocalization should get attention and reinforcement.
2. Giving form to the child's vocalizations; Putting the thoughts and feelings into words.
3. Giving models for what is to be said.
4. Responding to the child's actions with language.
5. Teaching imitation by imitating the child in play situations.
6. Encouraging the child's imitations.
7. Letting the child learn the *function* of language.
8. Helping the child with the *content* of language.
9. Not worrying him about the *form* of language at this early stage. The classroom teacher will do that later (Simmons-Martin, 1976).

HEARING AND HEARING AIDS

Ideally, in a parent–infant program there will be an educational audiologist as one of the professional staff involved with the total (re)habilitation program. This person, too, needs to work very closely with both the parent–infant facilitator and the parents and other family members. The parent-infant facilitator needs to learn from the audiologist the level and configuration of the child's hearing so that they together can make judgments concerning the intensity of signals that the child requires. The two professionals need to consult with each other concerning auditory programs, subsequent audiological evaluations, and possible changes in hearing aid settings or instruments. Parents, likewise, have a great need for the advice and services of the audiologist, for it is this professional who will be the consultant concerning all aspects of hearing.

The audiologist is the professional who should inform the parents of the child's hearing capacity, what he is likely to hear and not hear, the meaning of the audiogram, what the expectations of amplification may be, what the hearing aids can and cannot do, how to trouble shoot minor problems of the hearing aids, simple facts about amplification, the effects of ambient noise on the auditory signal, how to keep the hearing aids in their best working order, and all the other "physical" aspects of wearing hearing aids. More importantly, the audiologist should help the parents accept the aids and transfer this acceptance to the child. With young children, it is the parent, usually the mother, who must see that the child wears the hearing aids during all waking hours; it is she who must help the child become dependent upon the aids, to accept the aids as just a part of getting dressed every day.

Another task that often falls to the audiologist is that of explaining to the parents the nature of the child's hearing impairment. Even though an otologist has probably diagnosed the hearing impairment as sensorineural or conductive, or mixed, it is very likely that the parent has not grasped the full meaning of these terms during that early period of diagnosis. Parents need to know if any medical treatment or surgical procedure is appropriate, and if not, they need to have explained why surgery, chiropractic adjustments, acupuncture, or other procedures cannot restore the hearing that does not exist. It is natural for parents to want to explore all the possibilities, but they need kindly, authoritative advice as to which procedures can yield benefits.

SUMMARY

The concept of beginning intervention for hearing-impaired children during infancy, and involving the parents in this intervention, is an innovation in the educational process that appears to have reaped great benefits. Although there are no hard data yet to support this assertion, the fact that the children are being exposed to language, oral language, sign language, total communication, any language, at the appropriate time portends a more natural language-acquisition process than beginning the children in a program at three years of age, a time when most normally hearing children already have good command of the language of their culture.

The advent of parent–infant programs and the improved technology of sound amplification are two factors that can yield benefits for hearing-impaired children if the profession exploits these phenomena adequately. The rationale, the structure, and the goals of parent–infant programs have been discussed. The role and qualifications of the professionals and the activities of such programs have been described. Many such programs exist now, and some states mandate that services for hearing-impaired children be provided from birth on; this is certainly a step in a positive direction.

However, in developing strategies to assist parents in providing a productive language environment for their hearing-impaired children, professionals must bear in mind that parents of handicapped children, like their children, differ greatly, not only in culture, economic status, education, and intelligence, but also in the extent of their children's handicaps and abilities, and their readiness to adjust to the situation. Many forces impinge upon the parents at any given time. Rarely do any two or more sets of parents function at the same level at the same time. Thus each family group must be treated as a separate unit receiving individual guidance. Nevertheless, since they are all coping with a similar problem, the program should provide opportunities for group instruction and discussion. The primary objective of a parent–infant program is to help parents through a crisis period so that they can create an environment in which their child can acquire language in as nearly a normal process as possible.

REFERENCES

Bloom, B. (1964). *Stability and change in human characteristics*. New York: John Wiley & Sons.

Chomsky, N. (1980). On cognitive structures and their development: A reply to Piaget. In M. Piattelli-Palmarini (Ed.), *Language and learning : The debate between Jean Piaget and Noam Chomsky*. Cambridge, MA: Harvard University Press.

Erber, N. (1982). *Auditory training*. Washington, DC: Alexander Graham Bell Association for the Deaf.

Grant, J. (1972). *Proceedings of a workshop on the preparation of personnel in education of bilingual hearing impaired children, ages 0-4*. San Antonio: Trinity University.

Kagan, J., Kearsley, R., and Zelazo, P. (1980). *Infancy: Its place in human development.* Cambridge, MA: Harvard University Press.

Ling, D. (1976). *Speech and the hearing impaired child.* Washington, DC: Alexander Graham Bell Association for the Deaf.

McNeill, D. (1970). *The acquisition of language.* New York: Harper and Row.

Schlesinger, H. (1985). Deafness, mental health, and language. In F. Powell, T. Finitzo-Hieber, S. Friel-Patti, and D. Henderson (Eds.), *Education of the hearing impaired child.* San Diego: College-Hill Press.

Simmons-Martin, A. (1975). *Chats with Johnny's parents.* Washington, DC: Alexander Graham Bell Associaton for the Deaf.

Simmons-Martin, A. (1976). A demonstration home approach with hearing-impaired children. In E. Webster (Ed.), *Professionals approach parents of handicapped children.* Springfield, IL: Thomas.

Simmons-Martin, A. (1978). Early management procedures for the hearing-impaired child. In F. Martin (Ed.), *Pediatric Audiology.* Englewood Cliffs, NJ: Prentice-Hall.

Simmons-Martin, A. (1981). Acquisition of language by under-fives including the parental role. In A. Mulholland (Ed.), *Oral education today and tomorrow.* Washington, DC: Alexander Graham Bell Association for the Deaf.

CHAPTER 7

Early Education

The process of being educated begins at birth, with the parents as the first teachers, and continues throughout life. The parental role is normally an informal and casual one, and usually parents do not consider themselves teachers. However, with the hearing-impaired child it is imperative that the early learning period be structured so that the infant and toddler can receive the specific, contrived input necessary to compensate for the impoverished input that might otherwise be obtained due to the hearing deficit. Ideally, then, a hearing-impaired child's formal education begins very early in life, at home, and continues at the preschool age in a classroom situation. Even for normally hearing children, there comes a time when the home environment, no matter how substantial, is not enough; a child needs to be exposed to more than just his home.

Formerly, this time was judged to be at about 5 years of age, and kindergartens emerged to satisfy the growing needs of children for socialization and other positive gains a child receives through a kindergarten experience. However, there is currently a trend toward earlier exposure to so-called "formal" programs for all children, not only handicapped children. The new direction is probably the effect of many factors, but certainly prominent among them is the mounting evidence of the tremendous capacity for learning at the very early ages (Bloom, 1964; Kagan, Kearsley, and Zelazo, 1980; White and Watts, 1983 among others). Another factor, no doubt, is the entry of many mothers of young children into the work force at all levels of society (Washington and Oyemade, 1985). A third influence has been the attempt to close the achievement "gap" between lower socioeconomic-class and middle-class children by starting them in educational programs at an earlier age instead of the traditional kindergarten age (Bronfenbrenner, 1975). Thus, the last three decades have witnessed a plethora of early childhood programs of many philosophies and structures (Bereiter and Engelmann, 1966; Gray and Klaus, 1970; Karnes, 1969; Weikart, 1967, to name a few).

As mentioned earlier, preschool programs for hearing-impaired children are not new; they have existed for well over half a century. However, instead of being the exception, they are now commonplace, and most states mandate programs for all handicapped children from the age of three years. In the case of hearing and visual impairments, some states require programs from birth. The federal government has been very influential in promoting early childhood education for handicapped as well as nonhandicapped children. In the case of the former, credit for the impetus must be given the Handicapped Children's Early Education Program (HCEEP) in the Office of Special Education, U.S. Department of Education. This program has been instrumental in establishing and supporting experimental programs for young handicapped children with the purpose of encouraging their replication by local agencies (DeWeerd and Cole, 1976).

If one's philosophy is for hearing-impaired children to acquire language as nearly as possible, in the manner that hearing children do, then it follows that their home and educational environments should be as much like that of hearing children as feasible. This is not to say that hearing-impaired children will acquire language spontaneously in a rich environment; most need very special input from infancy for many years. Yet, a cursory examination of early childhood curricula and literature will reveal an overwhelming emphasis on language development for all young children, those privileged economically and intellectually as well as those deprived (Honig, 1982), including children with any handicapping condition.

In that case, the ideal early childhood program for hearing-impaired children is very similar to most early childhood curricula, with ample opportunities for learning in the cognitive, affective, social, and psycho-motor domains. In addition, there should be an appropriate balance of activities stimulating both the analytical and the creative hemispheres of the brain, with abundant experiences rich in linguistic stimulation, cognitive processing, symbolic play, problem solving, and creative endeavors. The away-from-home program must exceed even the very rich home environment in many important respects, or there would be no advantage to the early entrance into formal programs at the preschool age instead of waiting until the traditional kindergarten age.

Even for nonhandicapped children, there are many attitudes and skills that they can learn in a group setting that would be much more difficult to acquire in home situation. For example, social skills, such as taking turns, sharing time, attention, and materials with more than family members, engaging in group activities, to name a few, are elementary requisites for acceptable behavior within a group. Children can acquire early concepts of justice, compassion, and empathy with greater ease in group situations than otherwise. For handicapped children, the advantages are even greater. The skills and knowledge possessed by professionals trained in teaching handicapped preschoolers are used to great advantage in inducing or enhancing language acquisition, problem solving strategies, and the desirable social skills and attitudes already mentioned.

It is encouraging to note the attention which is being directed to the concept of integrating handicapped children with nonhandicapped children. The Head Start program has required that at least ten percent of its enrollment be handicapped children since 1975, and currently about eleven percent of Head Start children are handicapped (Washington & Oyemade, 1985). The misgiving that the normally developing children will not progress socially or cognitively at their natural rate when integrated with handicapped children has not proved to be so (Hanline, 1985).

A case in point is the program at Sunshine Cottage School for Deaf Children in San Antonio, Texas, which has maintained a "reversed mainstream" program for over a decade. Preschool-age normally hearing children attend classes with the hearing-impaired children on a daily basis. The classes are limited in size to four hearing children and four hearing-impaired children. Parents of both groups have voiced great satisfaction with the program. The parents of the hearing-impaired children have been pleased to see that their children can interact successfully with normally hearing children, and the parents of the hearing children have been pleased with the low teacher–child ratio, the enriched curriculum made possible by that low ratio, and other advantages not generally available under ordinary circumstances, such as frequent field trips. It is much more feasible to take eight children on a field trip than the normal-sized preschool class. However, perhaps the greatest advantage for the normally developing children is the sensitivity to and acceptance of individual differences that they acquire by developing friendships with handicapped children (Hanline, 1985). They learn that though their classmates have hearing and language deficits, they are very much like themselves. Longitudinal research is needed to determine the long-term effects for both the hearing and hearing-impaired children (O'Connell, 1984). It appears, then, that it is safe to say that there are benefits for children to reap from early education programs.

EARLY EDUCATION GOALS

The goals of education are continuous, and as stated earlier, the expectations for the child by all concerned parties should be congruous. Moreover, the goals for hearing-impaired children are not different from those for hearing children; the only difference is in the manner of attaining the goals. No goal can be achieved without the accompanying language. It is understood that the requisite language is an integral part of each goal. The fulfilling of this requirement is what differentiates an ordinary early education program from one for hearing-impaired children; for the latter, attaching language to all activities of the program takes on prime importance and becomes the heart of the curriculum. Furthermore, the general needs of children, as outlined in Chapter 1, must be incorporated into the designated goals and objectives of a program for hearing-impaired children. Instead of compiling a long list of very definitive objectives, let us consider three philosophical goals which can be adjusted to accommodate many different types of programs with children and parents of varying backgrounds.

Physical and Mental Health

The importance of good health, both physical and mental, for all children cannot be argued against. Although these two aspects of our total being appear to be quite separate, actually they influence each other to a great extent. A child who is chronically in poor health is very vulnerable to mental and psychological problems. By the same token, it is wise to investigate the physical condition of a child who has a poor self-image, lacks self-control, or manifests other signs of personality or mental disorders. Reaching this goal with hearing-impaired children has some special implications.

So far as physical well-being goes, all young children are predisposed to middle ear infections due to the horizontal position of the eustachian tube, which begins at the nasopharynx and opens into the middle ear, thus allowing upper respiratory infections easy access to the middle ear cavity. In the case of hearing-impaired children, such infections further reduce their hearing thresholds, exacerbating the impairment (Jaffe, 1977; Lim, 1977). A hearing child often can tell a parent or teacher when he has an earache, or a parent can notice when a normally hearing child is not hearing as well as usual. But the hearing-impaired child may lack the language to inform an adult of an earache or the depressed hearing threshold that frequently accompanies and follows a middle ear infection (Jaffe, 1977). Fluid in the middle ear, which is the cause of the reduced hearing acuity, is not always accompanied by pain, so the child or parent may not be aware of the problem. Teachers and parents must constantly be alert to this added danger to a child's hearing.

There are other threats to the physical well-being of hearing-impaired children. For example, bacterial and viral infections, such as meningitis and encephalitis, can cause hearing impairments to normally hearing children as well as exacerbating existing impairments and can bring on neurological complications as well (Hanshaw, 1976). In addition, excessively hyperactive children may need medication in order to function in a classroom. Teachers need to know of these conditions and know how and where to refer children who are in need of medical attention.

To promote good mental health may also take special measures. Parents and teachers may be hard put to explain to a hearing-impaired child why he cannot hear when other children, often siblings, and on occasion even a twin, can. Certainly, the child must come to the realization that he has a hearing deficit, but he must also be instilled with the desire and drive to fulfill his potential in spite of the handicap.

There are other threats to good mental health for a hearing-impaired child which do not apply to normally hearing children. For example, the former way be accused of a wrongdoing unjustly and may not have the language to explain his innocence. Repeated experiences of this nature can make a child distrust adults and peers. Teachers and parents must exercise caution in issuing admonitions and chastisements. Yet the same family and school disciplinary rules must be administered to both the hearing and hearing-impaired children in any group, for obvious reasons. It is indeed a difficult situation, and patience and good judgment are sorely needed. The health needs of the students, both physical and mental, are important considerations in the scheduling of daily activities, and every planned activity should comply with good physical and mental health practices.

Implicit in this goal is the social development of the child, the ability to be a contributing member of a group and to comply with classroom routines. Such ordinary encounters as sharing materials, caring for classroom pets and supplies, and helping with classroom chores, add to the child's sense of being a member of a group. Early experiences in making friends, participating in conversations, demonstrating leadership, cooperating with peers and adults on projects and in free play, are valuable lessons that will serve a child well all his life. This goal requires the cooperation of parents, as these efforts must have continuity away from school as well.

Logical Thinking and Responsibility

Given the proper conditions and assistance needed, young hearing-impaired children can learn to recognize dilemmas, to use logical means of arriving at resolutions, and implement their decisions into appropriate action. We must be sure to assign the children tasks for which they are responsible and encourage them to make decisions, even if the decisions are wrong on occasion (Figure 7-1). We must require that they answer questions by any means available to them; oral language or signs if such are adequate, or lacking those, gestures, pantomime, drawing, whatever is most favored. Then the teacher can attach verbal symbols to the expression and have the child repeat the utterance to the best of his ability.

Figure 7–1. *Anticipating what happens on the next page promotes logical thinking.*

This procedure, repeated often enough, will bring the child to the realization that he *can* make himself understood, and is capable of and is expected to respond to questions, to resolve problems, and to communicate with others. We need to ask even these very young children their opinions on matters that concern themselves and the total group; they need to have to devise alternative actions when their original plans go awry. Such practices occurring early in a child's life will help him become an adult who can think things through, predict outcomes, and accept consequences for his actions.

Cognitive Growth and Creative Expression

These two concepts might be considered to be quite disparate, since in general cognitive activity is a function of the left brain and creative activity a function of the right brain. However, there is one link that binds the two: language. Language and cognition are closely bound, and creative expression is one use of language. Moreover, every new expression an individual utters or comprehends is a creative act. There are other connections between cognition and creativity. For example, many problems of a cognitive nature require a creative solution, and a well rounded curriculum maintains a healthy balance of cognitive activities with ample occasions to solve problems, along with creative opportunities involving all the arts.

Implicit in this goal is the development of learning skills. The habits acquired at this early age will serve the learner well or deter learning all his life. Therefore, we want to instill habits of finishing tasks, of attending to a task in the presence of distraction, of seeking resources for assistance only when the child's own resources have been exhausted, and of deriving genuine pleasure from completing a difficult task.

Parents and teachers of hearing-impaired children can further this goal by offering generous, positive reinforcement when a child finishes a task successfully, by holding him responsible for completing the task even when other events were competing for attention, and by not assisting the child in a task if there is evidence that he can do it on his own. This does not mean that adults should not tender suggestions and advice when a child is stumped and seeks assistance.

To realize these skills the setting must be stimulating to the development of concepts, and must contain a variety of materials. There must be numerous opportunities for repetition and practice without producing boredom. In such a setting, the teacher must assess each child's progress often enough to know when to upgrade the tasks and materials, and expectations. We want our students to be challenged by the tasks we assign—the children should have to think hard and use their skills—but the tasks should be exciting and enjoyable. Learning does not have to be easy, but it has to be stimulating to qualify as fun.

PROGRAM CHARACTERISTICS

With these goals in mind, let us ruminate on the characteristics of a program for preschool hearing-impaired children. Instead of describing a program based on any particular "philosophy" (such as the behavioristic approach, the normal developmental approach, or the cognitively oriented approach), I prefer to discuss components of programs that could be called eclectic, adverting to all types of programs. In fact, in my years of teaching and observing preschool classes for both hearing and hearing-impaired children, I have been convinced that the "approach" is not as influencing a factor in a child's progress as the teacher's ability to adjust her philosophy and instructional techniques to the individual learning style and interests of each student.

Although at first individual consideration of each child appears to be an impossible task for a teacher of an entire class of preschool children, the children cannot be properly served without this requirement. Lindfors

(1980) recommends that the preschool teacher observe each child long enough to be able to discern three special interests, which enables the selection of language experiences that will be stimulating and will motivate the child to pursue these interests and learn the associated language in a most natural manner. Such a time-consuming task will have beneficial payoffs for a teacher of normally hearing children, but the benefits to a teacher of hearing-impaired children are multiplied many times over. Generally, classes for hearing-impaired children are much smaller than ordinary preschool classes, thus affording the teacher the opportunity for intense observation. Most states have guidelines and regulations concerning the teacher–child ratios in classes for handicapped children. Small classes for hearing-impaired children are essential, and the smaller the better, so long as there are enough children for interaction within the group.

Some of the requisites for optimum progress for the hearing-impaired early childhood student are a program with a well prepared teacher with four to eight students and a teaching assistant or aide, (if not full-time, at least part-time), an appropriate physical setting, and a flexible instructional design suitable for each child in the program. Needless to say, there must be a supportive administrative structure to coordinate the total setting.

Certainly, the staff must be aware of the significance of the milestone that the transition from home to school represents. This process is sometimes painful for both the parents and the child, especially since hearing-impaired children ideally begin classroom programs at an early age. The fact that the parents often cannot assure the child of their return can exacerbate the anxiety. Having the parent stay with the child can either ease the situation or prolong the adjustment; I've witnessed both positive and negative results with both strategies. If the child is familiar with the teacher, the building, and the other children, the adjustment is usually fairly smooth. In any case, the dichotomy between home and school can be lessened by having photographs of family members and pets in the classroom, stories read and books available about families and the various roles of the family members, by having projects that result in things for the child to take home, by keeping the parents informed about what is happening in the classroom, by having the parents keep the teacher informed about what is happening at home, and by encouraging the child to communicate to the parents what is done at school.

PRINCIPLES OF EARLY EDUCATION

It cannot be stressed too strongly that good teaching principles are the same for all children, whether they are normally hearing or hearing-impaired. Therefore, it remains for us to point out the difficulties of implementing some of the principles with hearing-impaired children and how to overcome the problems. As for all children, we want a program in which all components are integrated into a logical and developmental whole. According to Bloom (1964), children will demonstrate the greatest intellectual growth in the first four years of life. In addition, they will show rapid development in their motor abilities and affective behavior. We must take advantage of the optimum growth period to design programs that integrate their language, curiosity, problem solving abilities, creative talents, affective behavior, sensory capabilities, and motor abilities, into a planned and meaningful curriculum.

One notices immediately that language is at the top of the list and is involved in practically all the other activities. Therein lies the problem, and the difference between a program for hearing-children and one for hearing-impaired children. Language must be a focus of attention in any activity in the program. The teacher must translate the children's nonverbal activities into the verbal medium, using appropriate intonation and natural structure. For some unknown reason, there seems to be an impelling temptation among teachers of hearing-impaired children to use a rising intonation at the end of statements, resulting in a "sing-song" intonation rather than a natural one. This pitfall, and exaggerated lip and mouth movements, must be avoided. It is often necessary to phrase or rephrase a child's thoughts or actions so as to match the language to the activity, be it cognitive, creative, motor, or affective. This focus on attaching the verbal symbols to the action probably distracts the teacher and is the cause of the unnatural intonation. The teacher must carefully guard against such practices. However, providing repeated experiences that demonstrate the relation among objects and events to words, phrases, and sentences will enhance language and cognition, and is therefore a most important activity.

Concept Development

Remembering that language to accompany every activity is an inherent component to all principles governing early childhood programs, let us review some basic guidelines. If we endeavor to teach at the deep-structure level, one of our prime concerns is the growth of concepts. Children need to experience the same concept in different settings with different materials and different language. In other words, use different materials with the same concept, and use the same materials with different concepts. Slobin (1973) points out that when children first use new linguistic forms, they use them while expressing old functions, and when they first incorporate new functions into their language, they are expressed by old forms. We should incorporate this dictum into our programs by using new language with already established concepts, and by introducing new concepts with familiar language.

For example, the child will not develop the concept of *chair* from learning to pronounce the word, nor from learning that it is a combination of phonemes, nor that it is a noun with the features: common, count, inanimate, singular. Instead, the concept will emerge when the child apprehends that chairs come in many shapes, materials, colors, and uses. He will need to draw modifiers from many categories; chairs can be red, they can be big, comfortable, easy, straight, rockering. He needs to experience the concept of *chair* in various semantic relations as well; chair as the location (on the chair), chair as the instrument (with the chair), chair as the complement (broke the chair) and so on. If comprehension precedes expression, as many linguists attest (de Villiers & de Villiers, 1978; Edwards, 1974; Fraser, Bellugi, and Brown, 1963), this is the information that needs to be processed as the child is learning "chairness." A single encounter, no matter how exciting or successful, is not sufficient to build a sustained concept.

The young child must have many exposures from many views over a sustained period of time before a concept has some measure of stability. He needs a broad base of concrete, direct contact from which to abstract and generalize. The younger the child, the more sensory the contacts need to be. The direct encounters during play and other activities will afford the opportunity to infer the attributes of size, shape, color, texture, number, position in space, all the qualities that parents ordinarily label for their normally hearing children, and that teachers (and parents) must likewise do for hearing-impaired children. While we are building this concept of "chairness," a new concept, we can use concepts and language that are known to the child, for example, colors, shapes, size, materials, all the attributes and features that are familiar to him. Concepts of this nature are not built with questions such as, "Where is the chair?" We want our students eventually to be able to apply the word *chair* to abstract concepts, such as "to chair a meeting," or "to address the chair," or "an endowed chair." A kindergarten teacher of my acquaintance developed a unit on chairs in which she and the children investigated the origin of chairs, traced the evolution of their use and design from simple logs to ornate thrones, and studied their current prevalence. These children will have no difficulty in understanding the abstract uses of the word *chair*.

A Learning Model

The building blocks of concept development start with perceptions of concrete objects and events (Figure 7-2). From these perceptions, children form mental images that evolve into mental constructs and subjective ideas imaginatively structured (Nelson, 1977). The highest level of concepts allows for complex symbolism, generalization, and the ability to think abstractly, all of which are requisite to mature mental operations. A very simplified learning model could consist of only three components, input, process, and output.

Figure 7-2. *The building blocks of concept development start with perceptions of concrete objects and events.*

In the case of language, the linguistic input is matched to the child's sensory perceptions and thought. Because the auditory receiving system is defective and the child does not have the verbal label, the teacher will use imitation of the language as a means of assuring that there is linguistic input. The imitation serves an additional purpose; it integrates speech and auditory skills into the global communication process, and the teacher is assured likewise that the child is processing the linguistic symbols with the perception. This is especially important if the situation has been contrived by the teacher, who can be assured that the integrity of the child's thought is being maintained. The child processes the perception and at the same time the imitation is incipient output. The child imitates as best he can, matching the intonation pattern, the "time envelope," and what phonemic content he has control over.

The process aspect is the "deep structure," the "thought," the 'inner language" that the child is acquiring. The hearing-impaired child, like any child, will perceive many objects and events in the environment. The teacher cannot observe the processing, but she is in the best position to gauge what is being processed, since she has provided the input.

Output is what happens over time. Results are not immediate, and parents and teachers must not expect instant language. Breakdowns in output are most common in the functional use of language and can be observed in the context of the child's play and spontaneous utterances. The teacher then has a means of informal assessment that can guide in the evaluation of the extent to which the child has developed the concept. The hearing-impaired child's concept development may be well advanced beyond the ability to verbalize (Levine, 1981). Teachers and programs strive to close the gap between the two, for only when the child can manipulate his concepts by the use of verbal symbols can he take total advantage of his conceptual development.

Expressive Language

Another guiding principle is that of promoting and monitoring the children's expressive language. If we think of language as composed of function, content, and form, the teacher needs to keep these processes in mind while designing learning situations. There are many functions of expressive language, but high on our list of priorities would be for our students to be able to express personal needs, to express affection and love, to relate information, to seek information, to engage in social communication, to create prose and poetry, to control behavior, all the positive uses of language. The children will lead us to their immediate needs as they communicate with each other, their parents, and us. Along with the functions listed above are the pragmatics of linguistic discourse. They must know how to start a conversation, how to take turns conversationally, how to interrupt acceptably, how to address various partners, how much background to give the listener, all the pragmatic aspects of communication.

The content of what they have to say is our next concern. Parents tend to correct even very young children when they make mistakes in the truth value of their statements and ignore mistakes in form. Again, the experiences that the teacher contrives are most valuable, since she then can be confident that the input she provides matches the child's perception of the event, and that he is processing the language that parallels that percept.

The form of the output is our last concern, and with us as with the parents, the function and content should take precedence over the form. There comes a time when form will assume a high priority, but at the early stages of language emergence we are most interested in the transference of meaning, its appropriateness (function), and its truth value (content). Of course, if the form is so mangled that meaning is obscured, then it must be corrected, but never at the expense of spontaneity or originality. Many "incorrect" forms used by young children are charming and poetic, and reveal the level of conceptualization that the child is experiencing, a clue to the level of cognitive maturity, which can be of great value to the teacher.

Learning Skills

Overriding all principles is that of learning to learn. This principle has been implied and stated in respect to other aspects of early education, such as goals, objectives, and basic needs of children. True, it is a goal, but it is likewise a principle to be closely observed in all educational programs. Everything, every fact, every skill, every ability a child acquires in a program will be a waste of time if, during the process, the child does not become proficient in learning itself, or more important, does not develop a thirst for learning. He needs to gain organizational skills, inductive and deductive reasoning skills, and an enhanced memory capacity. The natural inclination is there; teachers and parents must be sure that it is not extinguished or diminished by constraining restrictions or rigid attitudes.

PHYSICAL COMPONENT

One of the most important aspects of the physical setting is that it should be a safe place where young children can explore, investigate, create, and interact with other children and adults. There should be few restricted zones that are off-limits to the children in their areas. The students should feel that all the areas are theirs to enjoy, use, and be responsible for. The literature is replete with suggestions and advice on physical settings for preschool children. In general, the main factors to be considered are (1) sufficient and appropriate materials, (2) adequate space, both indoor and outdoor, to allow for maximum freedom (within limits, of course), and (3) highly qualified adult personnel with whom the children can interact. The requirements in these respects are no different from those of normally hearing children and therefore will not be discussed further. Instead, let us consider what special needs the hearing-impaired child has so far as the physical component is concerned.

INDOOR AREA

First and foremost, the hearing-impaired child needs a quiet environment if sound amplification is to be effective. Air conditioning or heating units with excessive noise are to be avoided at all costs. This is sometimes hard to accomplish in old structures, or structures not readily adapted, but we are asking children to listen, or sometimes to learn to listen, at hearing thresholds. This feat requires concentration even in a quiet environment; it becomes close to impossible in a noisy one. If the building does not lend itself to sound absorbency, there are many things the staff can do to improve the setting; floors can be carpeted, windows can be draped or curtained, walls can even be carpeted, classes can be situated away from high-traffic areas and heating and air conditioning units, acoustical tiles can be placed over ordinary ceilings. If funds are available, acoustic engineers should be consulted as to the most efficient methods of making the indoor space as sound-absorbent as possible.

The more profound the hearing impairment, the greater the necessity for a quiet environment. It may be advisable for some children to use vibrotactile devices to afford additional stimuli. In such cases, the speech signal needs to be easily distinguished from environmental noise, which is not possible if there are competing signals.

There is a caveat in creating a completely sound absorbent environment, however. Somewhere the child must experience a "normal" environment; if mainstreaming into regular classrooms is the goal, a child will have to accustom himself to a less-than-ideal sound environment. Most public school classrooms, cafeterias, gymnasiums, and corridors are not sound-absorbent. On the contrary, they are quite noisy; the hearing-impaired child must learn to filter out everything but the important stimuli and attend to them. Certainly, a child who is anticipating entrance into a mainstream situation, whether in a preschool, elementary, or later setting, should have a great deal of experience in an ordinary, not highly absorbant, sound environment.

The indoor space should have adequate light for easy lip reading. While what the child hears, and can learn to hear, will be emphasized to the greatest extent possible, some profoundly hearing-impaired children must supplement the auditory input with visual input. As in the case of the acoustic environment, we want to make communication as easy as possible, not to add to the difficulties the child is already experiencing. Indoor space for all young children should be light and airy, but as with noise control, these factors are especially important with hearing-impaired children.

Another important aspect of the indoor physical environment is that there should be musical instruments that the children can play, in addition to any instruments that are part of the instructional program (such as a piano and a guitar that the teacher or assistants use). There must be easily accessible record players, tape recorders, Language Masters* or comparable machines, and any other equipment that will encourage the children to listen, talk, sing, or be involved in auditory and communicative activities of many kinds. There should be an abundance of visual stimulation as well. The children need to be exposed to novel displays so as to stimulate conversation and excitement. As with any early childhood classroom, there should be plants and pets that require feeding and care to be provided by the children.

For hearing-impaired children, it is most important that the environment be stimulating to communication. All good early education programs

---

*Bell & Howell Company.

emphasize communication skills, but with normally hearing children, these skills need only support; with hearing-impaired children, the skills need to be initiated, nurtured, and encouraged. Most early childhood programs have a housekeeping corner or some such area where children can pretend to be something or somebody they are not. Whether they pretend to be adults, animals, vehicles, or whatever, it is imperative that there be adequate space and materials to encourage symbolic play.

Normally hearing children do not start putting words together until they have virtually completed the sensorimotor period, and at the beginning of the pre-operational period, they are able to use both words and images to enhance their thinking (Streng, Kretschmer, and Kretschmer, 1978). Even if our students do not have the words (the verbal symbols), images or iconic representations help them to communicate their thoughts, and lead them to concept development. This ability to engage in symbolic behavior is a prerequisite to verbal expressive language. Whereas hearing-impaired children in early childhood programs are normally well beyond the sensorimotor period physically, they are not linguistically. Therefore, it is of even greater importance for symbolic activity of all types to be promoted in programs for hearing-impaired children.

Outdoor Area

The outdoor areas need to afford the same opportunities for hearing-impaired children as for all children. One of the most important factors in planning outdoor areas is for the children's safety. As with all programs, equipment needs to be sturdy and well maintained, and there may be additional requirements for hearing-impaired children so far as safety is concerned, because they may not hear warning signals and shouts. However, teachers and administrators should not be lured into overprotective measures, for the children must learn to compensate for their defective hearing by whatever means are necessary. Responsibility for their own safety should be fostered from an early age. For example, the outdoor play area offers a great opportunity for the development of self-discipline; the play area could have invisible boundaries with no fence. The children would learn not to exceed the boundary, not to chase a ball into the street, not to be tempted to leave the area for any reason. A fenced-in yard deprives the children of such responsibility and fosters dependence. Of course, a great deal of teaching is required to accomplish this control, and a great deal of close supervision is required while the concept is being acquired, but the payoff more than compensates for the time and effort expended.

This opinion is not shared by all teachers, administrators, and parents. There are negative consequeces for administrators if an accident should occur, and parents and teachers often want the security of a fence that cannot be scaled. Nevertheless there will be no protective fences later in the children's lives, and learning to stay within physical boundaries at school is a control that could be generalized to the home and possibly to nonphysical situations that will occur later in life.

The ideal outdoor play area promotes not only gross motor activity and physical growth, but also cognitive, creative, social, and communicative skills (Lovell and Harms, 1985). For example, children can develop from their outdoor play concepts of in–out, up–down, through–around, heavy–light, fast–slow, by means of gross motor activity that can be generalized to fine motor skills and even abstract concepts. They can observe the seasonal and weather changes; they can create with natural materials, sand, water, sticks; they can develop social skills as they learn to take turns and play cooperatively. These objectives are attainable for all children, but are especially valuable for hearing-impaired children when they learn to communicate about these activities. The time spent outdoors should be an integral part of the planned day. The outdoor activities should support and elaborate those which take place inside. If our students are to achieve to their full potential, we are obliged to provide the most advantageous physical setting for them (Frost and Henniger, 1979; Kritchevsky, Prescott, and Walling, 1969).

INSTRUCTIONAL COMPONENT

The instructional component is the area in which a program for hearing-impaired children differs the most from an ordinary preschool program. This is the area in which language, speech, listening, all the communication skills, are targeted for intense stimulation and practice. As mentioned earlier, these are important components of all early childhood programs, but they are the heart of a program for children with any kind of a language delay or deficit. Yet it is important that a program be designed for young children, not particularly hearing-impaired children. A child's needs as a child transcend any special needs as a hearing-impaired child, and the goals and principles of all programs should be guided by the basic needs first and foremost. It is difficult to create the atmosphere and program that will meet the special communication needs of hearing-impaired children and still have it remain a child-centered environment. The temptation is great to adapt elementary or kindergarten procedures to the preschool program and have little children sitting on chairs for long periods of time, filling out ditto sheets, or coloring within the lines. There are more suitable means of achieving the goals we seek, means whereby little children can do "little children" things, not the activities of older children adapted to them.

Bearing in mind the goals and principles already delineated, let us consider some guidelines to help us adapt objectives for normally hearing children to the needs of hearing-impaired children. The basic principles of constantly developing concepts, of promoting expressive language, of honing learning skills, all through a model of input, process, and output, are pervasive in our planning. However, the arrangement of the discussion to follow will vary slightly from that in the preceding section.

PHYSICAL WELL-BEING

The goal of physical well-being is commonplace for all preschoolers. What added dimensions are there for hearing-impaired children? Let us start with truly basic health concerns; personal cleanliness and grooming, good eating habits, ample physical exercise and fresh air, ample sleep and rest, adequate immunization and medical and dental check-ups, and control of contagious infections. Our students need to have information on all these subjects, but in addition, they need to have the language and the concepts which will enable them to contemplate and converse about them.

For instance, young normally hearing children often have esoteric signals for their bathroom needs; teachers need to know what signals their hearing-impaired students use at home, put them into verbal terms, and then be sure the children use them. It is not enough to point to the sink and expect the children to wash their hands; they must be expected to comply to the verbal command and respond with an appropriate comment according to each one's verbal ability, "I did," or "I will," or whatever. Just as the child's responses should vary, so should the command; it should not always be, "Wash your hands." The commands could very naturally be, on occasion, "Are your hands clean?" or "Did you remember to wash your hands?" or some such natural variation. Our students need more than one way to ask and answer questions; likewise they need to be able to comprehend and respond to the same question even though it may be couched in different terms. Very often, it is not the teacher who supervises the cleaning up before snack or lunch, so the teacher aide or volunteer must share the expectation that the children will respond verbally; consistency in demands is a firm requirement.

It goes without saying that the children need the actual words for the items of personal cleanliness—*soap, shampoo, towel, comb, toothbrush, sink, water, toilet*—in addition to the names of the parts of their bodies that will be involved with these items. It is not enough to know *finger*; they need to know *fingernail* (and know it has nothing to do with carpentry). It is not enough to know *leg* and *arm* unless they know that it is the *knee* and *elbow* that gets skinned so often. The nouns alone will not let them communicate what they are doing; they need the adjectives—*hot, cold, little, big, slippery*—and the verbs *wash, rinse, brush, comb, flush, turn on, turn off, dry*. Notice that some of the words serve in more than one capacity in everyday language: *comb* is commonly a noun and a verb; the same for *brush; dry* can be an adjective or a verb. We must *use* these dual functioning words naturally as verbs or nouns or adjectives just as the occasion demands. The only way our students will learn all the various uses of words is if they are exposed to them in the various contexts. Labeling the nouns, verbs, or adjectives will not help the children use them; we want functional language, not lists of words.

Another concern for the physical well-being of hearing-impaired children is the fact that the incidence of visual impairment is higher in this group than the national average (Calvert and Silverman, 1983). This finding should not come as a surprise, since the cochlea and retina are formed at the same developmental embryonic level, yet many hearing-impaired children's visual defects are not diagnosed and corrected (Moores, 1982). Teachers need to be alert to signs that their students may be experiencing visual difficulties. Excessive squinting, head turning to get an object in focus or in the line of vision, holding books or papers very close or very far from the face, are all indications that there may be visual problems. Any child may not realize that not everyone sees as he does, but a child with limited communicative skills is particularly vulnerable to having a visual impairment overlooked. Visual examinations are not always included in regular physical checkups, and undetected impairments can persist unless parents or teachers are aware of possible deficiencies.

Hearing children learn the names of foods without any tutelege, especially the foods they eat regularly. Our students must learn the proper names for foods. They must not call french fries "long yellow" or apples "red, round" or chocolate "brown." In addition to the correct names, we can teach even very young children about healthful and unhealthful foods. In this area the teacher needs to have close contact with the families to be sure that none is offended concerning their eating habits. Another caveat is to be familiar with the cultural background of each child. It would be improper to talk of a breakfast of juice, toast, and bacon and eggs to a child whose breakfast consisted of tortillas, chorizo, and mango; the latter is just as nutritious as the former. Again, we are striving for concepts, not lists of words. Thus these concepts will be developed in the natural context of snack time or lunch, a picnic, in symbolic play activities or, for older preschoolers, in a unit on food groups.

Physical activities give the teacher an ideal setting for group encounters which can promote team cooperation, social skills, and communication as well as physical fitness. The children can acquire concepts of patience as they wait their turns for the use of equipment, they can learn the difference between fantasy and reality as they pretend to be their superheroes, they can experience real team work as they play games or build trains or busses or castles. The physical activity period should be considered as much a part of the instructional plan as any other period.

For the teacher to have these objectives in mind does not mean that there should be no free play period. On the contrary, free play is most important, for this is the time that the children reveal their preferences for playmates, materials, and activities. There should be free play periods for both indoor and outdoor activities, for both active and quiet times. Teachers must observe carefully the free play so that they may attach the accompanying language to all the activities in which the children engage. Knowing each child's choices can help the teacher to provide the language that will serve in learning to communicate.

Most programs for young children provide for a quiet time, either on a mat or cot. The length and structure of this period should depend on the age of the children and the length of the school day. This period can be used instructionally to great advantage. In a half-day program, most children do not need to sleep, only to slow down for a short period. This is an ideal time for story telling or reading. Instead of encouraging the children to sleep, the time might be better spent in encouraging them to follow a story line, to anticipate succeeding events, and to draw inferences concerning the characters and their actions. If it is necessary for the children actually to sleep, play restful music on records or sing songs that the children know the words to; the rest and sleep the children get at home is probably more important to their general health than the comparatively short rest periods during the school day.

The importance of proper immunization and control of communicable diseases do not need justification, but certainly hearing-impaired children are due as much explanation as possible as to the necessity of covering their mouths during coughs and sneezes, of blowing their noses and keeping them wiped, of not drinking out of another's glass, of keeping their fingers out of their mouths, of not putting objects into their mouths, and all the other health admonitions. We want the best possible physical health for our students; their intellectual task, acquiring language, is a tough one, and they need all the physical strength they can muster.

Good Mental Health

This subject has been mentioned in several contexts, but it bears expanding in the context of the instructional aspect of a program for young hearing-impaired children. One of the most important elements of good mental health is a positive self-image. Often the self-image is a self-fulfilling prophecy, and a child accomplishes only what he perceives to be within his capabilities. A teacher can enhance or diminish a child's self-esteem in many ways. It is very important to anticipate a child's reaction to an admonition or chastisement, for depending on the child's personality and self-confidence, even a single cross word can be a crushing blow. When a child displays aggressive or disruptive behavior, a rule of thumb might be to let the punishment fit the criminal, not "the punishment fit the crime." Remember the dictum offered earlier that the child who deserves your attention and love the least needs it the most. True, children must learn to accept the consequences for their actions, but the kinds of accidents that happen in preschool classrooms—spilling paint or beverages, breaking equipment or even toileting accidents—are unintentional, and most children are already embarrassed and regretful. To scold a sensitive child or one with low self-esteem in front of others or even in private could certainly be damaging to an already insecure child. To encourage more caution, a teacher should have the child clean up the mess (if appropriate) and help repair the damage done, if possible, in as matter-of-fact way as possible. It takes close and thoughtful observation to assess the status of a child's mental health, but only through such observation can the teacher be confident of how to establish rapport with each child.

Children may be experiencing stress for any number of reasons; the parents' reaction to the diagnosis of the hearing impairment, too harsh or too permissive discipline at home, poor parenting skills in general, or marital discord, among others (Honig, 1986). Sometimes the children express their stress in subtle ways, and the teacher must watch for excessively aggressive or passive behavior, extreme dependence or avoidance of adults, or abnormal restlessness or drowsiness. A hearing-impaired child is not likely to be able to verbalize his stressful feelings; he may not even be aware that he is experiencing stress. Nevertheless, the stress will interfere with progress, and the teacher is obliged to mitigate the stress as much as possible.

One strategy is to help the child express these feelings by whatever means are available: verbally, with pantomime, through drawing. Another strategy is to structure the classroom routine to emphasize cooperation, not competition, so as to minimize the possibility of failure for the stressed child. Still another helpful technique is to read or tell illustrated stories of children who found ways to cope with various stressful situations (Honig, 1986). Often, role playing will help a shy child express stressful feelings, and by doing so reduce the stress. Sometimes a child can relate troublesome feelings that cannot be expressed in any other way through hand puppets. We must remember that hearing-impaired children react to the same conditions that normally hearing children do; the problem is intensified since they have fewer means of dealing with the destructive feelings due to their limited linguistic abilities.

Logical Thinking and Cognitive Growth

We want our students to become independent thinkers and learners. We can promote these activities by the kinds of questions we ask, by the kinds of questions we encourage the children to ask, by the examples of cognitive activity we demonstrate for our students, by the expectations we have for them, and by the motivation we instill in them. We should never answer a question which we could instead prod the students to answer for themselves. If our students grow up knowing that they can read meaningfully and find answers to their questions, perhaps we shall see fewer reports like the work of LaSasso (1986), who found that hearing-impaired children, more than normally hearing children at the same level, resorted to "visual matching" instead of comprehension when answering questions on reading material. We should be sure that all of the tasks we assign are exciting and challenging, not easy; learning should be fun, not necessarily easy.

Logical thinking can be encouraged by helping children in sequencing tasks, in serializing objects or even words by various categories, such as size or perhaps severity (Figure 7-3). In reviewing stories told or read to children, teachers should help them recall the events in a sequential order. Every class experience should be chronicled in some form—pictures, photographs, sentences—in the proper sequential order, and children should be able to sequence the episodes correctly.

Figure 7-3. *Logical thinking can be encouraged by helping children in sequencing tasks.*

Serializing objects for very young children can be accomplished with toys designed for that purpose or, more simply, with sticks or jar lids of graduated sizes, or pencils or crayons of different lengths, or even strips of paper. The concept can be elevated to a more advanced level by arranging adjectives in a serial order. For example, adjectives denoting size can be strung out from "wee" to 'gigantic." As the children acquire more descriptive terms, they can be inserted into the lineup in the proper placement. The children and teacher can discuss with words and concrete examples why a word belongs in a certain position. Concrete examples could be a ball the size of a pea to a beach ball, tea cups ranging from a cup from a tea set for a doll house to a Texas-size mug, books from the tiny Sendak books to a large unabridged dictionary. I have used wishbones from doves, quail, Cornish game hens, chickens, and turkeys with great success, especially around Thanksgiving. Activities like these help children realize that many adjectives are relative, not absolute. Such beginnings can generalize to abstract concepts such as *young–old, tall–short, near–far, expensive–cheap,* and other relative terms. Understanding that many adjectives are relative to the situation may have avoided the problem I observed once where a teacher had trouble convincing a 10-year-old hearing-impaired child that the older a person was did not necessarily mean the taller he was. She had to demonstrate with real people that a person in his 60s could be shorter than a person in his 20s.

We can help our students learn to think logically by monitoring the kinds of questions they ask. For example, in the game of guessing what is in the box or bag, if it is once ascertained that the contents are not something to eat, a question like, "Is is an apple?" should not be tolerated, and the questioner should learn why his question is inappropriate. The same principle holds for any other classification that would automatically eliminate certain questions.

There is a trend to teach logic and philosophy in the elementary grades and even the kindergarten. Studies have shown that children who have been in philosophy-for-children programs improved significantly in creative reasoning abilities, reading, and mathematics, compared to children who had not been in such programs (Brandt, 1982). Preschool children can apprehend the fundamentals of logic and philosophical thought by thought-provoking questions such as, "How do you know. . .?" or, "How did you figure this out?" We want our students to engage in persuasive discourse, both to be able to persuade, and to resist persuasion when based on false logic.

Many situations and activities which are part of the preschool routine can promote logical thinking. Such ordinary experiences as making predictions as to the content of the next page of a story being read, or guessing "what would happen if" the classroom hamster and turtle were put together, or what made the water in the refrigerator turn into ice, can cause children to engage in logical thinking. Goffin and Tull (1985) suggest that teachers consider certain principles when creating situations that will require the children to solve problems; the problems must be meaningful to the children to be worth the children's efforts to ponder them, they must be solvable at several levels of complexity (have more than one solution), they must be solvable by concrete means of information gathering, the steps toward solution must be observable so that the children can monitor their own actions, and they must be of the type that the children can evaluate their solutions.

Hearing-impaired children should be guided into metacognitive activities also, the ability to reflect about thinking, thinking about their own thinking. Wellman (1985) states that even very young children, 2- and 3-year-olds, perceive the difference between the mental world and the world of physical objects or behaviors. It is not beyond our students to know how they solved a problem and to be able to apply those processes to other situations, and not have to " reinvent the wheel" in every new situation (Gavelek and Raphael, 1985).

Problem solving is an area in which the teacher is obligated to engage the children. All kinds of problems are available in the preshool classroom: movement problems where a child can figure out different ways to move himself or to move objects; skill problems where a child must observe, hypothesize, and then act out on a problem; strategy problems where he must figure out the best of several alternatives to reaching a goal; and verbal problem solving, where the child verbally formulates solutions to a problem (Goffin & Tull, 1985). The last, of course, is the hardest for our students, but still we must aspire to this level. Teachers can serve as models as they solve problems themselves, contrived or not, and make the children aware of the process they are going through, and even request ideas from the children. A great deal of cognitive growth takes place when children recognize a discrepancy in the outcome of their actions as opposed to their anticipated results (Forman & Kuschner, 1983). We must be sure to allow the children the latitude to make such choices, especially in situations where there are alternate paths to follow. Goals of this nature are not beyond our students simply because they have hearing impairments. The children have these capabilities; they need only the language, the verbal symbols, to fulfill them.

Responsibility

Responsibility has been discussed in several contexts, but it is of especial importance in preschool classrooms. A project involving hearing 4-year-olds in such household tasks as setting the table, vacuuming the floor, sorting clothes, saving energy (turning out lights), cleaning the bathroom after a bath, and waking up to an alarm clock was undertaken by Wallinga and Sweaney (1985). They found, much to the surprise of the parents, that the children performed all these tasks willingly and with great vigor. The preschool teachers "taught" the tasks in the classroom and provided practice under their supervision before the children were to perform the tasks at home. The ripple effect of the positive results of the children's assistance with household tasks was that the children felt that they were productive members of the household, gaining in self-concept and independence. Naturally, the tasks chosen must be within the children's capabilities, and the children must be allowed all the time they need to accomplish their jobs.

Accepting and carrying out responsibilities is a characteristic that some adults do not have to an adequate degree. Preschool age is not too early to instill the concept, and the preschool class is an ideal setting for its initiation. Let us adults not underestimate the potential for learning and doing that young children possess.

TEACHING IMPLICATIONS

In other sections, discussion has centered on how children learn in a general way, citing the domains of learning, the sites of learning, the functions of each hemisphere of the brain, and the stages of learning or cognitive growth—sensorimotor, pre-operational, concrete operations, and formal operations. Some of the catalysts and strategies for learning have also been mentioned: motivation, experience, memory, imitation, practice, attending, and imagery. Early education goals and principles have been outlined to show how these form the basis for the physical and instructional components of a program.

It is important now to examine some ways to promote the kind of learning, especially language learning, that will serve hearing-impaired children in all the described areas. When children first begin to talk, they talk about themselves, their family members, and the important things in their lives, such as foods, baths, favorite toys, pets. These are highly perceptual and affective topics, and children are processing the items on the basis of the most salient perceptual features, often only one feature. This practice leads to overextensions, such as the young child's calling all men "Daddy," or all four-legged animals "dog" (Clark, 1973). Such occurrences are developmentally normal, and when they occur with hearing-impaired children, that is the teacher's cue that the child needs broader perceptual experiences, in order to base these concepts on a greater number of perceptual features.

Therefore, the early experiences parents and teachers provide for hearing-impaired children should be highly perceptual and affective. Even though preschool-aged hearing-impaired children are no longer in the sensorimotor stage of development so far as nonlinguistic development is concerned, they have not outgrown their need for sensory stimulation, nor are they functioning linguistically at their chronological level. Let us then inundate them with activities that will stimulate their sensory equipment and assist their integration of these perceptions into concepts. But most importantly, let us assure that linguistic symbols are attached to the concepts. The research reported here gives evidence that the following sequence is the natural one, and the omission of any segment would result in language learning at the surface structure level only, with no base structure to support it cognitively.

Planned Experiences

In a sequential program, all hearing-impaired children would begin with language motivating experiences selected by virtue of the children's need for acquiring and broadening concepts and for developing the language that makes the concepts manipulative and retrievable. The experiences should be selected so that the children will talk as much as possible using spontaneous, appropriate language. Much of the activity might appear to be "unstructured," but the teacher must know why the activity is introduced. The teacher must remember also the functions of language the pupils must be able to use: language for communication, language as a cognitive tool, and language as an outlet for creativity. Another factor influencing the instructional plans is the need for a balanced program, one that will stimulate both hemispheres of the brain. This may seem like a formidable and impossible task, but such is not the case. True, not every experience can promote all these operations, but wonderful and exciting combinations can be achieved.

In choosing experiences, the teacher should consider whether or not the experience is (1) interesting enough to elicit spontaneous language from the children, (2) simple enough that the children can participate physically as well as observationally, (3) simple enough to be completed in a reasonable length of time, (4) flexible enough that children of various levels of development will all benefit from it, (5) whether it relates to everyday experiences so that the language and knowledge acquired can be generalized to other situations, (6) whether it will relate to specific concepts being introduced or developed in another area, and (7) whether or not it will be fun for the teacher as well as the children. It goes without saying that the teacher should have specific language, cognitive, social, and creative objectives for every experience planned.

One of the best barometers to use in choosing experiences for young children is to follow the children's interests, and the easiest way to ascertain their interests with any confidence is to observe the children in their free play and listen to their "conversations." Note the activities that hold their attention when it is not necessarily so directed; note what they relate to each other, by whatever means they are capable of; note the kinds of books that attract them; note which toys receive the greatest wear; note the activities that arouse the keenest competition for materials or resources. If teachers of young children would use their students as "curriculum guides," they would achieve great strides in language development, since there would be no problems with motivation, attention, or appropriateness.

Experience as the Vehicle for Learning Language

Such an ordinary experience as popping corn can satisfy many of the requirements for learning listed above. The children will involve their sensory capacities as they feel the unpopped kernels of corn, hear the kernels popping, smell the corn during the popping process, and taste the popcorn with and without salt. However, the most important step is often neglected: the children must acquire the language to describe the process. Critical to linguistic development at this stage is the kind of linguistic data provided, and the "provider." There must be an adult who offers language to be imitated by the child in any fashion he is capable of. The imitated form will probably be telegraphic. Nevertheless, this reduced imitation should be reinforced through the adult's encouraging acceptance and the provision of an expansion to the child's telegraphic form. The child has the opportunity to contrast his imitation with the model at the near instant of presentaton. Finally, the auditory feedback, however minimal, plus the kinesthetic feedback of producing the utterance, serve as additional reinforcers.

Even though the literature reflects doubt as to the effectiveness of expansion as a promoter of language growth (as opposed to making a comment on the child's utterance) (Cazden, 1972), there is evidence that parents naturally expand their children's telegraphic utterances (Brown, Cazden, and Bellugi, 1969). It is highly important for the hearing-impaired child to hear the expanded, corrected form of the utterances, and special care should be exercised to ensure the integrity of the child's meaning.

The role of imitation in language learning is likewise unclear, but the literature does suggest that imitation can play a role in the learning of new words and new grammatical constructions. It has been reported that some normally hearing children use imitated new words in already learned constructions, and others use new imitated constructions with already learned vocabulary (Bloom, Hood, and Lightbown, 1974). Teachers may not know which strategy certain children are using to acquire language, but they may use imitation of their modeled sentences as a technique with some degree of confidence, assuming that they are promoting vocabulary growth or grammatical structures, or, "serendipitously," both.

Another teaching strategy that we can glean from the literature is that of recasting the children's utterances into more complex forms. For example, when a child makes a comment, the adult often responds with either a question relevant to the comment, or rephrases the comment in a more complex or more correct form (Nelson, 1975). Remembering that novelty and stimuli more complex than the level at which the child is functioning can be highly motivating, we want to be continually alert to natural opportunities to increase the children's language power.

For example, in the popcorn experience just described, the teacher would elicit language from the children during the entire experience, in addition to having them participate physically to the greatest extent possible. They could measure out the popcorn, pour it into the popper, pour in the oil, and salt the finished product. One of the spontaneous comments might be, "Popcorn hot." The teacher would then expand the utterance to, "Yes, the popcorn is hot," and have the child imitate the sentence. Then she might add (1) a question form, "Oh, did you burn your mouth?" or (2) the more difficult form, "You didn't burn your mouth, did you?" or (3) another difficult form, "Yes, be careful not to burn your mouth," or (4) "Be careful or you'll burn your mouth," or (5) "Wait until it cools before you eat it," or (6) the very difficult, "Don't eat it until it's cool," or any number of other sentences depending on what the current objectives are for any particular child. If the teacher is trying to establish past tense questions, she will ask (1). If she is working on tag questions, she will ask (2). If she is emphasizing variations of the negative, she will ask (3). If she is trying to establish the disjunctive *or*, she will ask (4). If she is working on relative clauses of time, she will ask (5). If she thinks this child can comprehend the reversed chronology of (6), she will try it. The teacher must anticipate the spontaneous language that the children are capable of, and be alert to opportunities to elevate that level.

The above discourse involves using language as a means of communication. To stimulate the children to use language cognitively, the teacher will ask the children what made the popcorn pop, why it did not pop immediately, why some of the kernels did not pop, why we needed oil; where the oil went; if this corn is the same kind that we eat on the cob or from the can or the freezer package. With luck, the children will have questions for the teacher to answer.

There is an affective component in this experience too. The children should be happy to take turns doing the various chores. They should be happy to share the popcorn equally among all the members of the class and the adults present. They should want to help with the cleanup. They should be pleased with each other's questions and encourage any reticent classmates to express themselves. They should feel that this experience has been a group experience for all to enjoy.

This same experience could qualify as a stimulator to both hemispheres of the brain. The left hemisphere, the analytic and verbal processor, would have been stimulated by the cognitive activity just outlined, while the right hemisphere, the one dealing with imagery, spatial concepts, and creativity, would have been stimulated as the teacher helps the children to recall the experience using imagery, pictures (both the children's and the teacher's), in addition to the verbal symbolism, in both oral and written forms.

An even more versatile experience would be a kite flying experience. Even if the children are too young to make their kites, they can take part in the motor activity of running fast enough to get it up into the air (psychomotor), they can be helped to figure out what carried it to such heights (cognitive), and they can experience joy at their success or disappointment at their failure at the kite's demise as it gets snagged in a tree (affective). The children will use language to communicate their activity to each other, to their parents and others, to mediate the cognitive function, and to create a story about their experience. They will have used language in three functions. They will be activating their left hemispheres as they determine the direction of the wind, as they use verbal language to describe the event, as they analyze their success or failure. They will be activating their right hemispheres as they recall the experience using imagery to assist in the recall, and perhaps in making a graphic representation of the experience.

This is not a far-fetched experience, and is one that could be designed to stimulate children of all ages. Older children could design and build their own kites, measure wind velocity to determine a good day for the activity, investigate sites for optimum flying, devise a means to measure the string as it is let out in order to determine the height of the kite, have a contest to see who could estimate the height most accurately, compare the heights attained on a very windy day as opposed to those on days with less wind, or determine the function of the tail and how to adjust its length according to the wind velocity. A creative teacher can use such experiences with practically any age children, at any language level, and fulfill objectives in all learning domains, using language for multiple functions, and stimulating both hemispheres of the brain. Contrast the above experiences with the less exciting, less functional, and less relevant traditional "news" of reading about someone named Johnny (unknown to the class), doing something with someone (also unknown to the class), at a place unknown to the class. Or imagine the "thrill" of mastering such phrases as, "Susie has brown eyes," "Tom is absent," "Jack has an apple in his lunch," "It is raining'" or "Today is Tuesday!"

The kinds of experiences that are available to young children are limitless. Even very young children can deduce simple scientific principles if provided with hands-on contact with the facts. There is great excitement in seeing a magnet attract iron filings or paper clips, and seeing what it cannot attract, in watching a moth spin a cocoon or a spider spin a web, seeing baby chicks peck their way out of shells after turning the eggs for 21 days, noticing the difference in the growth of sweet potato vines when one is placed in a bright location and another is placed in a dark space. A highly manipulative science project can stimulate children to talk fluently and to use logical thinking in expressing their ideas to a greater extent than a "language arts" period can (Rowe, 1978).

A wholesome and effective introduction to sex education could occur by observing a pair of hamsters mate and subsequently deliver a litter of hamsters. The housekeeping corner can promote a great variety of social growth and functional language as children take the roles various characters. They can be helped to develop metalinguistic awareness as they learn to use different registers for talking to their "spouses," their "children," their "friends." Also, the teacher is very likely to learn a great deal about the language and child-rearing practices the children are exposed to at home by what is observed while the children play. These and hundreds of other experiences can be carried on without leaving the classroom and with very little financial expenditure on equipment. The experiences cited here are only examples of the learning that can be extracted from experiences if they are selected wisely with definite objectives in mind.

The Chart Story

After the actual experience, the teacher will put it in permanent form by writing a description of it on a large piece of tagboard, thus creating a "chart story." Even though the teacher has either written or mentally planned the anticipated story, it cannot be presented until after the experience. More than once, I have had the entire focus of attention diverted from my objectives to a totally unexpected aspect of an experience. For example, after a trip to the pet store, the purchased goldfish died before the anticipated story could be presented. Another time, a flat tire eclipsed the mission of a field trip. These unexpected occurrences can produce prolific spontaneous language and should be exploited, not ignored.

The language of the chart story should be natural to the situation. It should be as nearly as possible the kind of language a hearing child would use to relate the events to peers or parents. There should be a variety of language constructions, sentence lengths, and sentence types—simple and complex, descriptive and exclamatory. Children love to see their names in print, so generally every child's name will appear on the chart. Start each sentence on a new line to help the children develop the concept of a complete utterance. Illustrate every sentence in some manner, with a drawing, a stick figure, or a photograph (Figure 7-4). Just as children like to see their names, they like to see pictures of themselves, so photographs used to illustrate the sentences are very popular. The text should include both new and old words and new and old constructions. A good guide are the strategies used by some normally hearing children as they acquire language: use new words in old constructions; use known vocabulary in

Figure 7-4. *The teacher focuses on auditory input.*

new constructions (Slobin, 1978). Include language constructions and vocabulary from previous chart stories that need to be practiced, but be certain to upgrade each chart in some aspect.

The Genesis of Literacy

There is research that attributes reading skills to certain oral language skills. Snow (1983) describes the difference between contextualized literacy skills as opposed to context-free abilities. The former include the ability to read familiar items such as one's name, the slogan on a T-shirt, or the name of a cereal on the cereal box. The latter would include the ability to read words completely out of context, such as reading a novel where the viewpoint of the author or another must be assumed, which is the kind of reading that is eventually required in the middle elementary grades.

Snow states that certain types of oral language can prepare children for this level of literacy. To help prepare for reading, children should be encouraged to talk about the past, repeat shared events, and tell stories about remote events not in the immediate environment. Teachers do this very thing when they require children to recall past experiences recorded as chart stories. The follow-up work that accompanies chart stories could be very helpful in generating the ability to talk of noncontextualized events. The work could start with very concrete and personal events and then procede to related topics that the experience suggests.

We teachers of young hearing-impaired children face something of a dilemma. On the one hand, one of our most overriding objectives is to help the children use to the greatest extent possible their residual hearing, no matter how minimal. To accomplish this, we must make the child aware of what he is able to hear, and not have him depend solely or even primarily on visual input. We want the child to become dependent on hearing, not vision for primary language stimulation. Some children are so profoundly hearing-impaired that this goal is unrealistic, but the technological advances in the past two decades have brought high quality auditory stimulation to hearing aid users not previously possible (Ross, 1986), and have made it possible for many hearing-impaired children to develop speech through the auditory feedback loop (Pollack, 1984). On the other hand, a high level of literacy is one of our ultimate goals for hearing-impaired adults. This latter has been and continues to be an indictment against the efficacy of education of hearing-impaired individuals, when 15- to 18-year-old hearing-impaired students are reading at an average of a third- to fourth-grade level, depending on the assessment instrument used (Quigley and Kretschmer, 1982; Quigley and Paul, 1986).

There are currently a number of reports in the literature of the "untaught" reading and writing abilities of young children (Bissex, 1980; Cazden, 1981; Chomsky, 1981; Jenson, 1985; Read, 1971; Schickedanz, 1986; Snow, 1983; Vukelich and Golden, 1984). As noted earlier, the preschool class is not place for little children to engage in drills using fine muscle skills or sit quietly for long periods of time. However, according to the current reports, some of the products young children are turning out are far from drill work and show great promise of fine literary skills (Figure 7-5).

Schickedanz (1986) states that literacy has its roots in infancy, and that oral and written language support each other. She reports that as adults do not expect children's first attempts at talking to be adult-like, they should not expect early writing to be in adult form, and that the childish swiggles and lines are, nevertheless, early composition and have been overlooked as such. She explains that for literacy to proceed naturally, the environment must support it by means of adults who mediate print in a positive fashion. She states further that "experience with books in the preschool years is

Figure 7-5. *Computers are great promotors of literacy.*

related to successful literacy development during the elementary school years" (p. 37).

Vukelich and Golden (1984) point out that many young children know the difference between drawing and writing, and cite illustrative literature demonstrating the fact. Another interesting finding is that the "writing" of these young children resembles the written forms of their cultures. For example, the Saudi Arabian child's "swiggles" look Arabic, the Israeli child's resemble Hebrew symbols, and the American child's look like cursive writing (Dahl, 1985). Moreover, some preschoolers have been able to "read" what they have written, showing that they understand that written symbols carry meaning. Vukelich and Golden recommend that teachers of preschool children provide a center for writing (with materials such as paper, crayons, pencils, felt-tip markers, as well as typewriters, magnetic and wooden letters) with daily opportunities and time for writing.

Chomsky (1981) asserts that children need to have experience writing with their own invented spellings before they are expected to read. She warns that adults must not judge correctness from their standards, but rather from the child's level of experience with literate material. For instance, it is correct for a child to spell *karate* CRIT, since all the sounds in the word are represented (the /ai/ contains the /a/ sound and the letter *t* accounts for the last syllable). She suggests that teachers encourage writing, and alerts them to some of the deviations to expect: missing short vowels (e.g. *dog* is likely to be spelled DG); TR and DR will be written CHR and JR; short vowels may be altered (/ey/ for /ɛ/). This early writing helps the child make the association between the spoken and written symbol, and the associations are all the more meaningful when the child arrives at them himself.

Some of the invented spellings reported by Chomsky appear also in Bissex's report (1980) of her son's learning to write and read. He developed the two skills in tandem and reported to his mother that "once you know how to spell something, you know how to read it" (p.5). The question of reading, a receptive language skill, as a prerequisite for writing, an expressive skill, was certainly refuted in this case. Read's report (1971) that most of his subjects learned to spell before they learned to read adds more credence to the notion that writing can precede or occur simultaneously with successful reading.

The studies cited were all concerned with normally hearing children who were developing oral language in a natural sequence. Are these findings applicable to hearing-impaired children? I think so. Truax (1978) reports that spoken language aids the learner in the process of learning to read and write. Is it possible that the advantage works in both directions; that the ability to read and write aids in the acquisition of expressive language? I think this possibility deserves serious consideration and investigation. While our prime concern is communication, expressive and receptive, by means of inferring the language "rules" of English, there is no substitute for good reading skills; a person can read at a much faster rate than he or she can listen or talk. Think of the enormous amounts of linguistic data a person can process through reading as opposed to listening. The average speaker speaks at a rate of about 135 words a minute (Modisett and Luter 1984), and though there is no "best" reading rate, (the rate depends on the task and the material), an average reader can read most material two to three times faster than the speaking rate (Smith, 1971).

If our students can become efficient readers, and learn to enjoy reading, there is great hope that their use of language can approach that of normally hearing individuals. Most classrooms for preschool hearing-impaired children are replete with written symbols—the children's names, chart stories, calendars, bulletin displays—and certainly recognition of these written forms are the beginning of reading. However, there are no reports to my knowledge of research concerning projects with hearing-impaired children with great emphasis on free, not structured, writing as a prelude to reading.

Some researchers might warn against such practices at the very early ages for fear of developing habits of visual rather than auditory dependency (Ling, 1976; Pollack, 1984). Others might think such writing skills are beyond the capabilities of young hearing-impaired children because the skills are dependent upon matching written symbols to sounds that are often distorted or unintelligible for our students. However, we cannot afford to ignore the successes reported in the literature. We aspire to language facility and literacy for hearing-impaired children, and early writing experiences have proved to reap beneficial results with hearing children. We should at least investigate the possibilities for preschool hearing-impaired children. Quigley and Paul (1986) report that high academic success of hearing-impaired children is attributable to adequate verbal language abilities; any activities that support the enhancement of these abilities must be encouraged. It could well be that early writing experiences can contribute to such success. Longitudinal studies following hearing-impaired children who have had such experiences into the upper elementary grades would be most revealing as to the benefits of such programs.

SUMMARY

This chapter has been concerned with early education programs for hearing-impaired children. Ideally, children would come into such programs after outgrowing parent–infant programs. Obviously, this is not always the case. Therefore, the teacher must assess the entry level of each student and plan accordingly. If the child is at the very earliest stages of language development, the teacher must begin with primitive linguistic patterns, but always adjust for the fact that the child is not an infant. Goals and principles of early education have been outlined and applied to the education of young hearing-impaired children, and the physical and instructional components of a program have been presented. The importance of concept development, expressive language, and the attainment of good learning skills has been emphasized. The emergence of concepts through first-hand experiences has been stressed as a means of promoting logical thinking and cognitive growth. Finally, the implications of these goals and principles for teaching have been discussed, along with a suggestion that early writing may be a promoter of good reading skill and the acquisition of verbal language abilities.

REFERENCES

Bereiter, C. and Engelmann, S. (1966). *Teaching disadvantaged children in the preschool*. Englewood Cliffs, NJ: Prentice-Hall.

Bissex, G. (1980). *Gnys at wrk: A child learns to write and read*. Cambridge, MA: Harvard University Press.

Bloom, B. (1964). *Stability and change in human characteristics*. New York: John Wiley & Sons.

Bloom, L., Hood, L., and Lightbown, P. (1974). Imitation in language development: If, when, and why. *Cognitive Psychology, 6,* 340–420.

Brandt, A. (1982, September). Teaching kids to think. *Ladies Home Journal,* pp. 104–106.

Bronfenbrenner, U. (1974). *A report on longitudinal evaluations of preschool programs* (Vol. 2). Washington, DC: DHEW Publication No. (ODH) 76-30025.

Brown, R., Cazden, C., and Bellugi, U. (1969). The child's grammar from I to III. In J. Hill (Ed.), *Minnesota symposium on child psychology* (Vol. 2). Minneapolis, MN: University of Minnesota Press.

Calvert, D. and Silverman, S. (1983). *Speech and deafness.* Washington, DC: Alexander Graham Bell Association for the Deaf.

Cazden, C. (1972). *Child language and education.* New York: Holt, Rinehart, and Winston.

Cazden, C. (1981). Language and learning to read. In C. Cazden (Ed.), *Language in early childhood education.* Washington, DC: National Association for the Education of Young Children.

Chomsky, C. (1981). Write now, read later. In C. Cazden (Ed.), *Language in early childhood education.* Washington, DC: National Association for the Education of Young Children.

Clark, E. (1973). What's in a word? On the child's acquisition of semantics in his first language. In T. Moore (Ed.), *Cognitive development and the acquisition of language.* New York: Academic Press.

Dahl, K. (1985). Research on writing development: Insights from the work of Harste and Graves. In R. Kretschmer (Ed.), *Learning to write and writing to learn. Volta Review, 87,* 35–46.

de Villiers, J. and de Villiers, P. (1978) *Language acquisition.* Cambridge, MA: Harvard University Press.

DeWeerd, J. and Cole, A. (1976). Handicapped children's early education program. *Exceptional Children, 43,* 155–157.

Edwards, M. (1974). Perception and production in child phonology: The testing of four hypotheses. *Journal of Child Language, 1,* 205–219.

Forman, G. & Kuschner, D. (1983). *The child's construction of knowledge: Piaget for teaching children.* Washington, DC: National Association for the Education of Young Children.

Fraser, C., Bellugi, U. and Brown, R. (1963). Control of grammar in imitation, comprehension, and production. *Journal of Verbal Learning and Verbal Behavior, 2,* 121–135.

Frost, J. and Henniger, M. (1979). Making playgrounds safe for children and children safe for playgrounds. *Young Children, 34,* 23–30.

Gavelek, J. and Raphael, T. (1985). Metacognition, instruction, and questioning. In *Metacognition, cognition, and human performance* (Vol. 2). Orlando, FL: Academic Press.

Goffin, S. and Tull, C. (1985). Problem solving. *Young Children, 40,* 28–32.

Gray, S. and Klaus, R. (1970). The early training project: The seventh-year report. *Child Development, 41,* 909–924.

Hanline, M. (1985). Integrating disabled children. *Young Children, 40* (2), 45–48.

Hanshaw, J. (1976). Cytomegalovirus infections. In F. Top and P. Wehrle (Eds.), *Communicable and infectious diseases.* St. Louis: Mosby.

Honig, A. (1982). Language environments for young children. *Young Children,* 2 (38), 56–67.

Honig, A. (1986). Stress and coping in children (part 2). *Young Children, 41,* 47–59.

Jaffe, B. (1977). Medical evaluation and medical management of children with sensorineural hearing loss. In F. Bess (Ed.), *Childhood deafness: Causation, assessment and management.* New York: Grune & Stratton, 1977.

Jensen, M. (1985). Story awareness: A critical skill for early reading. *Young Children, 1,* 20–24.

Kagan, J. Kearsley, R. and Zelazo, P. (1980). *Infancy: Its place in human development.* Cambridge, MA: Harvard University Press.

Karnes, M. (1969). *Research and development program on preschool disadvantaged children: Final report.* Washington, DC: U.S. Office of Education.

Kritchevsky, S. Prescott, E., and Walling, L. (1969). *Planning environments for young children: Physical space.* Washington, DC: National Association for the Education of Young Children.

Levine, E. (1981). *The ecology of early deafness.* New York: Columbia University Press.

LaSasso, C. (1986). A comparison of visual matching test-taking strategies of comparably-aged normal-hearing and hearing-impaired subjects with comparable reading levels. *Volta Review, 88,* 231–238.

Lim, D. (1977). Infectious and inflammatory auditory disorder. In F. Bess (Ed.), *Childhood deafness: Causation, assessment and management.* New York: Grune & Stratton, 1977.

Lindfors, J. (1980). *Children's language and learning.* Englewood Cliffs, NJ: Prentice-Hall.

Ling, D. (1976). *Speech and the hearing impaired child: Theory and practice.* Washington, DC: Alexander Graham Bell Association for the Deaf.

Lovell, P. and Harms, T. (1985). How can playgounds be improved? *Young Children, 40,* 3–8.

Modisett, N., and Luter, J. (1984). *The basis of voice and articulation* (2nd ed.). Minneapolis, MN: Burgess.

Moores, D. (1982). *Education of the deaf: Psychology, principles, and practices* (2nd ed.). Boston: Houghton Mifflin.

Nelson, K. (1975). Individual differences in early semantic and syntax development. In D. Aaronson and R. Rieber (Eds.), *Developmental psycholinguistics and communication disorders. Annals of the New York Academy of Science, 263,* 132–139.

Nelson, K. (1977). The conceptual basis for naming. In J. Macnamara (Ed.), *Language learning and thought.* New York: Academic Press.

O'Connell, J. (1984). Preschool integration and its effects on the social interactions of handicapped and nonhandicapped children: A review. *Journal of the Division of Early Childhood, 8,* 38–48.

Pollack, D. (1984). An acoupedic program. In D. Ling (Ed.), *Early intervention for hearing-impaired children: Oral options.* San Diego: College-Hill Press.

Quigley, S. and Kretschmer, R. R. (1982). *The education of deaf children.* Baltimore: University Park Press.

Quigley, S. and Paul, P. (1986). A perspective on academic achievement. In

D. Luterman (Ed.), *Deafness in perspective*. San Diego: College-Hill Press.

Read, C. (1971). Pre-school children's knowledge of English phonology. *Harvard Educational Review, 41,* 1–34.

Ross, M. (1986). A perspective on amplification: Then and now. In D. Luterman (Ed.), *Deafness in perspective*. San Diego: College-Hill Press.

Rowe, M. (1978). *Teaching science is continuous inquiry*. New York: McGraw-Hill.

Schickedanz, J. (1986). *More than the ABCs*. Washington, DC: The National Association for the Education of Young Children.

Slobin, D. (1973). Cognitive prerequisites for the development of grammar. In C. Ferguson and D. Slobin (Eds.) *Studies in child language development*. New York: Holt, Rinehart and Winston.

Slobin, D. (1978). A case study of early language awareness. In A. Sinclair, R. Jarvella, and W. Levelt (Eds.), *The child's conception of language*. New York: Springer-Verlag.

Smith, R. (1971). *Understanding reading: A psycholinguistic analysis of reading and learning to read*. New York: Holt, Rinehart and Winston.

Snow, C. (1983). Literacy and language: Relationships during the preschool years. *Harvard Educational Review, 2,* 165–189.

Streng, A., Kretschmer, R., and Kretschmer, L. (1978). *Language, learning, and deafness*. New York: Grune & Stratton.

Truax, R. (1978). Reading and Language. In R. Kretschmer and L. Kretschmer (Eds.), *Language development and intervention with the hearing impaired*. Baltimore: University Park Press, 1978.

Vukelich, C. and Golden, J. (1984). Early writing: Development and teaching strategies. *Young Children, 2,* 3–8.

Washington, V. and Oyemade, U. (1985). Changing family trends-Head Start must respond. *Young Children, 40,* 12–19.

Wallinga, R. and Sweaney, A. (1985). A sense of real accomplishment. *Young Children, 41,* 3–8.

Weikart, D. (1967). *Preschool intervention: A preliminary report of the Perry Preschool Project*. Ann Arbor, MI: Campus Publishers.

Wellman, H. (1985). The origins of metacognition. In D. Forrest-Pressley, G. MacKinnon, and T. Waller (Eds.), *Metacognition, cognition, and human performance* (Vol. 1). Orlando, FL: Academic Press.

White, B. and Watts, J. (1973). *Experience and environment*. Englewood Cliffs, NJ: Prentice-Hall.

CHAPTER 8

The Role Of Creativity In Learning

Fostering creativity in instructional programs has been advocated for decades in the professional literature (Bruner, 1961; Fromm, 1959; Guilford, 1959; Marksberry, 1963; Taylor, 1964; Torrance, 1964). These investigators, among many others over the years, have postulated that creativity is an essential element in adapting successfully to changes in one's environment, and its development provides a means by which the individual can approach the problems that life presents. The extent to which the admonitions of these investigators have been heeded in educational programs is debatable.

However, in the case of hearing-impaired children, the issue is a most important one. Not only do our students need such an expedient to cope with the environment, they need extra-linguistic avenues of expression since they commonly have restricted verbal communicative abilities. The arts are the most available vehicles, especially for young children. They do not necessarily require a great monetary investment; many materials are abundant and inexpensive. The raw materials from which children can create are commonplace. They can draw or paint with few materials, dramatize with few or no props, sing or recite with no accompaniment, or can dance with or without accompaniment. Each of these areas can be greatly embellished with props, supplies, and musical instruments, but the point is that the avenues of creativity exist in even the most austere conditions. Therefore, creative expression is a realistic objective even for very young children.

Gardner (1982) comments on the remarkable artistry demonstrated by preschool-aged children in painting and sculpting, music, poetry, dance, all the arts. He comments further on its disappearance in the elementary years. One wonders whether this transition is due to outside influences (adult or peer pressures) or simply if it is a by-product of the advance from the pre-operational stage to that of concrete operations. During the elementary years, children are expected to learn to conform to rules and to engage in logical thinking. It may be that their submission to these conventionalisms inhibits or possibly extinguishes their creative talents, sometimes for the rest of their lives. Research reports indicate that creativity, especially in the form of imagination, drops off after the age of five or six (Gardner, 1982; Torrance, 1964). If so, there is all the more reason that concerted effort be expended to facilitate its manifestation in the preschool years in hopes that some of it will reappear during adolescence, the formal operations stage.

As teachers, we must be certain to reward creative achievements and help the creators take pride in their products. We must not equate intelligence with creative ability, for there is little relationship between the two (MacKinnon, 1971; Torrance, 1964). Martha Graham, the highly acclaimed dancer and choreographer, has been quoted as asserting that everyone is born a genius; it is only a matter of how long a person is allowed to keep this gift before it extinguishes or is squelched. If Graham is correct, teachers and parents of young children have a heavy obligation to help children retain their genius qualities.

We must not be too restrictive in our conception of creativity. For an act or product to qualify as creative, it need not be an earth-shaking discovery, nor a product eligible for a Nobel Prize. There are probably as many definitions of the word as there are writers, but certain descriptors persist. The words *new* and *novel* appear frequently, and often creativity is associated with problem solving. Bruner (1962) adds the element of surprise in addition to novelty in his definition, as well as a more common form of creativity, discovery (1961). While preschool children are not likely to produce creations that will surprise the world, they certainly can discover many natural phenomena and surprise themselves with their discoveries. On the basis of their discoveries, even little children can rearrange or transform their original perceptions into new and more sophisticated concepts. Such a definition implies that creative experiences are available to anyone at any level of development (Grant, 1979).

CREATIVITY AND THE ARTS

Often the arts come to mind when contemplating creativity, and as previously mentioned, the arts are an area that are particularly available to young children. Art, music, drama, dance are all activities that fit appropriately into curricula for young children. However, Brittain (1979) suggests that the arts component of a curriculum should have as its objective the development of the total child, not some isolated skill such as a preparation for reading. All the activities must be appropriate to the physical and mental capabilities of the children, and the children have to have had sensory experiences with materials and objects before they can be expected to represent them in any art form. Again, we are reminded of the necessity for firsthand experiences, and the more sensory, the better.

The Visual and Plastic Arts

So far as painting, drawing, and sculpting are concerned, the necessary materials may be simple or elaborate depending on the resources of the program. The most important factor is that they should be readily available to the children (Figure 8–1). They should be within easy reach, require little cleanup, and should not be limited to use at a certain time of day. They should be as varied as possible; crayons, brushes, felt-tip pens, paints, chalk, clay, scissors, glue, and of course, paper are the more essential items (Brittain, 1979). The literature in early childhood education contains ample descriptions and accounts of high quality art programs for young children (Dimondstein, 1974; Franks, 1979; Gardner, 1982; Lasky and Mukerji, 1980; Smith, 1983; Sparling and Sparling, 1973; Taunton, 1984). The

Figure 8–1. *Materials should be readily available.*

principles and objectives described by these researchers are highly applicable to hearing-impaired children. What our students express in their drawings, paintings, clay sculptures and the like are forms of communication. We should respect them as such and provide the verbal attachments that will enable the children to convert their artistic ideas into the verbal mode of expression.

There are specific strategies which adults should use, and some to avoid, when discussing children's art with them (Schirrmacher, 1986). The opportunities for rich verbal dialogue can be enriched or diminished by the comments adults make. If our comments are always complimentary but perfunctory, children will not be stimulated to describe or discuss their work. By the same token, if our comments, even though sincere, are always the same—"Oh, that's great!"—they too will no longer carry meaning. To ask a child, especially a hearing-impaired child, what he has created can be abortive to a conversation as well. He very likely cannot put into words the emotions of the moment, especially if he feels lonely or ignored for some reason. Or if he has had no particular theme in mind, he may feel that his work is not worthwhile. The child may be in the same situation as Isadora Duncan when she stated, "If I could say it, I wouldn't have to dance it" (Gardner, 1982, p. 90).

A less abrasive attempt at eliciting information on what the child is expressing is a gentle probing approach where the teacher gives the child a choice of what he wants to divulge about his creation. A probe such as, "Do you want to tell me something about this?" gives the child an option of discussing his work on his own terms. We want to be careful not to place our judgment above the child's, or give the child the impression that we are requiring a "story" about every artistic endeavor engaged in (Schirrmacher, 1986). The best time to talk about a child's work is probably immediately after it is finished. Dimondstein (1974) warns us not to look for representation in children's art, but instead attend to design qualities, shapes and forms. Talk about their use of color, texture, patterns, and the like.

Young children's remarkable ability to express themselves through painting, drawing, and sculpting is as prevalent among hearing-impaired children as with hearing children. It may take some special skills on on the part of teachers to transform the ideas expressed into verbal terms in the case of hearing-impaired children, and it is important to respect children's wishes so far as explanations of their creations are concerned. On the other hand, if a child is eager to share his feelings, this is an opportune time for the teacher to provide the necessary linguistic data, and at the same time help the child realize that there are multiple means of expressing oneself, and that words are useful in many contexts.

Symbolic and Dramatic Play

Symbolic and dramatic play are important ingredients in a child's cognitive, linguistic, and social development. A child must be able to represent persons, objects, and events in his mind before he is able to form concepts; he must have the ability to let one element, a word or phrase, represent a concept before he can put the words to use. The child must be able to recognize family and group relationships, and his representation in these groups, before he can become a participating member of any group.

Symbolic or imaginative play offers children the opportunity to use dramatization, imitation, experimentation, transformation of objects and animals into fanciful artifacts, new uses of language, leadership abilities, among endless other possibilities, to promote cognitive, language, and social growth.

Creative thought can be facilitated through playing with objects. Trostle and Yawkey (1983) report that because the child first lives with concrete objects, activity with these objects are the precursors to his thought processes. They state further that the child's playing with these objects in exploration, repetition, replication, and transformation lead to creative thought. The operations proceed from simple to complex and from concrete to abstract. During the explorative stage, the child examines the object and learns its various uses. In repetition, he practices the functions of the objects and thereby learns more of his physical world. In the replication stage, the child uses objects to reconstruct "real" articles that he knows, such as a house. In the final stage, transformation, the child actually thinks creatively as he transforms the forms and functions of the objects in his life. He now is engaged in symbolic play.

Adults play an important role in helping the children advance from stage to stage. According to Trostle and Yawkey, teachers must recognize three important elements in creative thought: internal reality, internal motivation, and internal control. Children must be allowed and encouraged to suspend reality and imagine "what if" situations: In internal motivation, the ideas must come from the child or a peer group, and not an adult. Internal control dictates that the child be the director in the execution of the activity. Within these guidelines, an adult can provide materials, suggest expansions on the child's original ideas, and encourage other children to join in the project. In the case of hearing-impaired children, the teacher's main role very likely is to provide the accompanying language.

Gardner (1982) outlines the development of children's imaginative play, beginning with the time when the 1-year-old follows the parents around the house imitating their activities. At this level, the child may become the "doer" as he feeds his doll or puts it to sleep. He may even advance to having the doll carry out adult functions. This level Gardner calls selective imitation, where the activites have little variation or modification. While this is certainly symbolic activity, it does not represent the quality of imaginative play that follows. In later stages, the child can imitate an event in a context other than its natural one. Later still, he can substitute one object for another; for example, a stick for the vacuum sweeper. By the age of 3 and a half or 4, he can use substitutes for the agents as well as the objects of his play; the agent can be a doll or some such substitute. The highest level is obtained when a group of children participate in such play agreeing on all the substituted items and the roles each will portray.

Gardner (1982) points out further shifts in young children's play. Around 4 years of age, children are not as dependent on concrete objects and other individuals in their dramatic play as formerly. They shift to dependence on language to support their fantasies, and narration rather than props take the lead. Immediately, we are aware of the gulf in linguistic sophistication which separates hearing and hearing-impaired children. Teachers and parents must be observant enough to notice this shift and supply the language that is needed. The astute teacher will know what imaginative activities are going on in the classroom and will contrive a way to introduce the appropriate language for the children, perhaps at a later time so as not to interrupt the play. Here we have another example of the discrepancy between the normal development in an area, that of imaginative play, and our ubiquitous problem, language competency.

Music and Dance

Hearing-impairment alone does not eliminate the ability to enjoy music, either as a performer or as a listener. Students at Sunshine Cottage School for Deaf Children in San Antonio have been attending the children's concerts performed by the San Antonio Symphony for many years. With the cooperation of the Symphony, high fidelity FM amplifying equipment is installed whereby the students receive an undistorted signal, and even the profoundly hearing-impaired students report that they enjoy the music very much. Also, in my years of teaching and observing hearing-impaired children, I have noticed that some children have a very fine sense of rhythm even without any training, and others can develop good rhythm with instructions. Good rhythmic ability has long been recognized as a support for intelligible speech (Calvert and Silverman, 1983), and programs for hearing-impaired children have traditionally included rhythm and music periods for the students.

The advanced technology in sound amplification has made music a much more available art form for hearing-impaired children than formerly. The Dallas Regional Day School for the Deaf has had an orchestra of children playing Carl Orff instruments in a highly sophisticated fashion. These are inner-city children who probably would not have the opportunity to play a musical instrument were it not for the school program. Hearing-impaired children are also capable of singing, maybe not with as much pitch variation as hearing children, but in perfect rhythm and with great enjoyment. The same is true for dance; hearing impairment is no handicap to dancing in all forms, from classical ballet to square dancing. I once taught a group of teenagers who memorized the calls in a square dancing routine and did not even need to hear nor lipread the calls for the changes; they attended only to the music and its rhythm.

In addition to its role as a support for rhythmic speech, music has other important values, even, or rather especially, for hearing-impaired children. The neurological seat of music is believed by many to be in the right hemisphere of the brain, as opposed to that of speech and language in the left brain (Gardner, 1982). Instead of exerting logical or analytical activity (left brain functions), music induces feelings; tensions, contrasts, balance, abstract concepts (Langer, 1942). This stimulation affords a nonverbal method of communicating, both receptively and expressively for hearing-impaired children. By listening or producing various forms of music, the students may be able to respond to other's abstract feelings or express their own, a feat perhaps not possible with words. Considering the difficulty they have with verbal language, every alternative is welcome.

What about singing for hearing-impaired children? Of course, the amount and configuration of the child's hearing impairment will dictate to a great extent the ability to carry a tune, but all gradations of tunes exist. Intonation is so important in carrying meaning and in aiding intelligibility in discourse, that singing, in even very primitive forms, needs to be given serious consideration. Ling (1976) and Calvert and Silverman (1983) discuss the importance of intonation in developing speech for the hearing-impaired. Singing cannot help but be a benefit to speech. Bernstein (1976) speaks of music as being innately endowed, as language is, and cites the infant's remarkable range of pitch in his earliest babbling as an example. No doubt, some children are more musically talented than others, but if all children have an innate capacity for music, let us teachers exploit it to the fullest extent. Even if the children are not able to carry a recognizable tune, they should know the joy of "saying" a song in time to the music, alone or in a chorus.

LANGUAGE AS AN AVENUE OF CREATIVITY

The use of language as a means of creative expression has been alluded to several times throughout this work, yet one may wonder how language can be a creative tool for hearing-impaired children when they have such difficulty with it. Furthermore, in a teacher's zeal to focus on the communicative functions of language for hearing-impaired children, there can be a tendency to overlook its value as creative expression. As with talent in the visual and plastic arts and imaginative play, young children evidence unusual creative gifts with language. Not only hearing children, but hearing-impaired children come up with charming and artistic utterances. A hearing-impaired child once described Dr. Max Goldstein, the founder of Central Institute for the Deaf in St. Louis, as his spark plug, meaning his inspiration and mentor; another once referred to a drawer as the table's pocket (Grant, 1979). Such utterances certainly qualify as metaphors, since the children's intent was to attribute a quality of one object to another object (or person). Such expressions are creative in the truest sense of the word, and in some respects, hearing-impaired children are more likely than hearing children to use them, since the former group is not as inhibited by the "rules" of discourse as are hearing children once they reach the stage of concrete operations, the elementary years (Gardner, 1982).

Keeping such abilities functioning can aid in the later use and understanding of figures of speech, especially metaphor and proverbs. Figures of speech such as similes, metaphors, and idioms are difficult structures for hearing-impaired students to use and to understand (Israelite, Schloss, and Smith, 1986). This lack of facility with these structures contributes to the notion that hearing-impaired individuals are literal minded and cannot handle abstractions. Moreover, students cannot enjoy literature and poetry unless they can be comfortable with figures of speech. Teachers of hearing children are encouraged to use strategies to enable their students to cast aside their learned linguistic restrictions so that they may express themselves in creative channels such as poetry and imaginative writing. In contrast, hearing-impaired children are generally not as constrained linguistically as normally hearing children, and thus should be more comfortable in artistic literary forms. If, as little children, they are exposed to nursery rhymes, fairy tales, poetry, and prose and are encouraged to tell and dramatize stories, real and fictional, then the ability to enjoy both reading and writing in these forms when they are older should be feasible.

In planning curricula for preschool hearing-impaired children, the arts should be considered an integral part of the instructional component, not a good activity if there is time. The arts are a natural and appropriate means through which a child can grow in cognitive, language, and social skills, and expression in any art form is high powered symbolic behavior. Children, especially young children, have an affinity for the arts, and educators should consider this bonding an advantage to be put to use.

COMPUTERS AS AGENTS OF CREATIVITY

Time was that the first thought that came to many eduators' minds when the use of computers in the classroom was mentioned was drill and practice. Some dubbed them "expensive workbooks" and other such derogatory terms. Others, who were not quite so hostile to the idea, might include tutorials as one function of the classroom computer. However, many of these programs, too, had their critics who disapproved of the lack of student interaction. However, drill and practice and tutorials do not begin to describe the capabilities of the microcomputer in the classroom; moreover these are the more mundane uses of the computer (Peterson, 1984). There are not many educators now who deny the possibilities of microcomputers as positive learning tools, and most of them are no longer hostile, even though they may not be enthusiastic.

The use of microcomputers with young children and their use with handicapped children is no longer rare, and reports of successful projects appear frequently in the literature (Burg, 1984; Goldenberg, Russel, and Carter, 1984; Graham, 1984; Hart-Davis, 1985; Lange, 1985; Rushakoff, 1984; to name only a few). Today's children are very comfortable with machines of all kinds; coin operated vending machines, laundry machines, and video games, among others. Computers are not that unusual; there are built-in computers in everything from automobiles to toys. Moreover, in some respects, the computer is self-motivating in that children can spend long periods of time at a computer and not become bored. In projects with young students at Sunshine Cottage School for Deaf Children, the students have argued over their turns at the computers when there were not enough for each student to have his own. Certainly, "time on task" is as important a requisite for learning as is motivation, and the computer qualifies as a positive force in each instance.

Computers, like many technological advances, can promote or inhibit learning depending on how they are implemented. If the computer, or television, or films, or film strips, or any educational "tool" is used to lure children into complete passivity, it is not contributing toward a child's development in any domain; it is a time-waster or a babysitter. However, used correctly, the computer has remarkable features. For instance, programs can be designed especially for certain children with specific objectives in mind. Teachers can prepare individualized computer programs for children who lack self-confidence, for children who have particular difficulties in a certain area (e.g., hand–eye coordination), for children who have personality problems. To tailor programs for individual children, teachers must learn programming techniques and not rely completely on commercially prepared materials (Burg, 1984). However, a teacher does not have to be a computer whiz to do this; there are authoring programs which make it possible to develop a program with a minimum of computer knowledge. Just as one does not have to know how an automobile engine works to drive a car, a teacher does not have to know everything about the computer to use it to advantage.

The greatest value of computer experience for hearing-impaired children is that they must communicate with the computer, and communicate in a manner that the computer can understand (Figure 8-2). The machine is very unforgiving; a missing comma or space can render an "error" message. This may appear to present an unsurmountable obstacle for hearing-impaired children, but quite the opposite is true. There is a computer language, LOGO, especially designed for children, and it has been used with young hearing-impaired children quite successfully (Grant and Semmes, 1983).

Papert, its author, (1980) describes this language as a tool to facilitate higher-level thinking in children. Some of the advantages of LOGO are that the child is in control; he designs the program. While instructing the computer, the child is thinking about thinking, his own thinking and the computer's "thinking," how the computer will use the commands he is issuing. He is engaging in metacognition, a process necessary for many types of cognitive functioning and leading to abstract thought processes (Herbert, 1982). Metacognition is a key component in reading, also, especially reading to learn, a skill which will play a vital role in a child's later years (Armbruster, Echols, and Brown, 1982).

Figure 8–2. *Hearing-impaired children learn to communicate with the computer.*

LOGO uses metaphor in its language along with other structures parallel to human language (e.g., vocabulary, syntax, recursive properties) which could conceivably generalize to a child's communicative competence. As he uses the recursive capabilities of LOGO, he can induce the recursive properties of language, the ability to insert one phrase or clause within another ("The boy who hit the girl lives next door").

The use of relative clauses, for example, is a difficult concept for hearing-impaired children, both in reading and in expressive language (Russel, Quigley, and Power, 1976). If they learn to maintain their own (or another's) thought from the subject of an utterance, past the inserted thoughts, to the final resolution, they will have mastered the recursive property of language. The analogy with LOGO is that to get from the start of a program to its resolution, the programmer has the option of inserting supporting commands, not unlike the recursive properties of English, which facilitate the execution of the program. Another parallel to English is the ability to conjoin one procedure to another very much like the coordination of one word, phrase, or clause to another in English. The development of these concepts can generalize to expressive and receptive communication.

In addition to LOGO there are single-keystroke programs based on LOGO which are popular with little children. A program called *Little Logo* (Semmes and Hutcherson, 1984) has been used quite successfully with young hearing-impaired children at Sunshine Cottage School for Deaf Children. In this program, a child needs only to strike one key on the keyboard to obtain an entire command. For example, when the child strikes *F* the cursor, or "turtle," moves a designated number of spaces forward. No keyboard skills are required, although after a short period of time, the children were using two hands and most of their fingers on appropriate keys rather than only index fingers "hunting and pecking." Little Logo provides an easy transition to regular LOGO. Yet in Little Logo the children learn to develop hypotheses, to test them, and to predict outcomes. They experience serialization as they command sequences and repeats. They apply reversibility as they correct their errors. These are processes that will facilitate the transition from the pre-operational stage of cognitive development into the concrete operations stage. The children in this project became so comfortable with the computers that one day when one of the youngsters saw a picture of a typewriter, she shouted, "Oh, computer!"

Some researchers have reservations about the value of LOGO or its simplified forms for preschool children (Brady and Hill, 1984). They feel that having the commands preprogrammed may be premature, and that the children should have adequate skills for programming before they engage in it. On the contrary, the experience at Sunshine Cottage was that the children gained knowledge in areas not ordinarily accessible to young children; knowledge of right and left, the value of numbers (their sequence), spatial relationships, and relative size, are only a few of the concepts that were developed during the project. Perhaps the greatest gain was that the children thoroughly enjoyed themselves and were proud of the designs, patterns, and pictures they created.

There are numerous commercially available progams for preschool children; there are even special keyboards with oversized keys with pictorial representations on them to denote their various functions. As computer hardware becomes less and less expensive, perhaps it will become more prevalent in preschool settings. The children are ready for computers; the adults need to catch up (Figure 8–3).

SUMMARY

As stated at the beginning of this chapter, all individuals have creative abilities, but children, especially young children, have exceptional abilities, and these need to have the opportunity to be expressed. Children naturally express creativity through the visual and plastic arts, through drama and imaginative play, through music and dance, and through language. In

Figure 8–3. *Children are ready for computers.*

addition, children today can express their creative ideas through computer experiences. Teachers of hearing-impaired children should provide the same opportunities for creative expression as do teachers of hearing children. Time spent in the arts should not be considered "extra-curricular." Time spent in the arts or other creative endeavors promotes growth in social, cognitive, affective, and linguistic domains; it could not be better spent.

REFERENCES

Armbruster, B., Echols, C. and Brown, A. (1982). The role of metacognition in reading to learn: A developmental perspective. In R. E. Kretschmer (Ed.), *Reading and the hearing-impaired individual.* Washington, DC: Alexander Graham Bell Association for the Deaf.

Bernstein, L. (1976). *The unanswered question.* Cambridge, MA: Harvard University Press.

Brittain, W. (1979). *Creative art and the young child.* New York: Macmillan.

Brady, E. and Hill, S. (1984). Young children and microcomputers: Research issues and directions. *Young Children, 39,* 49–61.

Bruner, J. (1961). The act of discovery. *Harvard Educational Review, 31,* 21–32.

Bruner, J. (1962). *On knowing.* Cambridge, MA: Harvard University Press.

Burg, K. (1984). The microcomputer in the kindergarten. *Young Children, 39,* 28–33.

Calvert, D. and Silverman, S. (1983). *Speech and deafness.* Washington, DC: Alexander Graham Bell Association for the Deaf.

Dimondstein, G. (1974). *Exploring the arts with children.* New York: Macmillan.

Franks, O. (1979). Scribbles? Yes, they are art *Young Children 34,* 15–22.

Fromm, E. (1959). Creativity. In H. Anderson (Ed.), *Creativity and its cultivation.* New York: Harper and Row.

Gardner, H. (1980). *Artful scribbles: The significance of children's drawings.* New York: Basic Books.

Gardner, H. (1982). *Art, mind, and brain.* New York: Basic Books.

Goldenberg, E., Russel, S., and Carter, C. (1984). *Computers, education and special needs.* Reading, MA: Addison-Wesley.

Graham, L. (1984). The use of microcomputers for the remediation of learning problems in children with communication disorders. *Journal of Childhood Communication Disorders, 8,* 79–88.

Grant, J. (1979). Experience: The foundation of language acquisition. In A. Simmons-Martin and D. Calvert (Eds.), *Parent–infant intervention: Communication disorders.* New York: Grune & Stratton.

Grant, J. and Semmes, P. (1983). A rationale for LOGO for hearing-impaired preschoolers. *American Annals of the Deaf, 128,* 564–569.

Guilford, J. (1959). Traits in creativity. In H. Anderson (Ed.), *Creativity and its cultivation.* New York: Harper & Row.

Hart-Davis, S. (1985). The classroom computer as a partner in teaching basic skills to hearing-impaired children. *American Annals of the Deaf, 130,* 410–414.

Herbert, C. (1982, August). Thoughts about thoughtful play from the player's point of view. Paper presented at the American Psychological Association National Conference, Washington, DC.

Israelite, N., Schoss, P., and Smith, M. (1986). Teaching proverb use through a modified table game. *Volta Review, 88*, 195–207.

Lange, M. (1985). Using the turtle tot robot to enhance LOGO for the hearing impaired. *American Annals of the Deaf, 130*, 377–392.

Langer, S. (1942). *Philosophy in a new key*. Cambridge, MA: Harvard University Press.

Lasky, L. and Mukerji, R. (1980). *Art: Basic for young children*. Washington, DC: National Association for the Education of Young Children.

Ling, D. (1976). *Speech and the hearing-impaired child: Theory and practice*. Washington, DC: Alexander Graham Bell Association for the Deaf.

MacKinnon, D. (1961). Educating for creativity. In G. Davis and J. Scott (Eds.), *Training creative thinking*. New York: Holt, Rinehart and Winston.

Marksberry, M. (1963). *Foundation of creativity*. New York: Harper and Row.

Papert, S. (1980). *Mindstorms*. New York: Basic Books.

Peterson, D. (1984). Will education be different (better) in the year 2,000? *Popular Computing, 3*, 10–18.

Rushakoff, G. (1984). Microcomputer assisted instruction in communication disorders. *Journal of Childhood Communication Disorders, 8*, 51–61.

Russell, W., Quigley, S., and Power, D. (1976). *Linguistics and deaf children: Transformational syntax and its applications*. Washington, DC: Alexander Graham Bell Association for the Deaf.

Schirrmacher, R. (1986). Talking with young children about their art. *Young Children, 41*, 3–7.

Semmes, P. and Hutcherson, L. (1985). *Little logo*. Dallas: Lonestar.

Smith, N. (1983). *Experience and art: Teaching children to paint*. New York: Teachers College Press.

Sparling, J. and Sparling, M. (1973). How to talk to a scribbler. *Young Children, 28*, 333–341.

Tauton, M. (1984). Reflective dialogue in the art classroom: Focusing on the art process. *Art Education, 37*, 15–16.

Taylor, C. (1964). *Creativity: Progress and potential*. New York: McGraw-Hill.

Torrance, P. (1964). Education and Creativity. In C. Taylor (Ed.), *Creativity: Progress and potential*. New York: McGraw-Hill.

Trostle, S. and Yawkey, T. (1983). Facilitating creative thought through object play in young children. *The Journal of Creative Behavior, 17*, 181–189.

CHAPTER 9

Bilingualism and
the Hearing Impaired

There exists another minority within the minority of hearing-impaired children that must be addressed. What of the children from homes where the language spoken is not English? In other chapters, I have stressed the importance of abundant linguistic input in order that the infant and young child should have ample data from which to infer the grammatical rules of the language. What if the language at home where the infant spends the bulk of his life is different from the one of the parent–infant facilitator or the teacher? How effective can the parent–infant facilitator be if she must counsel with the parents through an interpreter? These and other questions are very troublesome and deserve serious thought.

Some may want to shrug off this problem as a minor one that exists only in a few geographic areas of the nation. However, the minority racial and ethnic numbers in the United States are increasing at a staggering rate. It is estimated that by the year 2,000, there will be nearly 40 million inhabitants of non-English-speaking backgrounds in the nation (NACBE, 1981). The Annual Survey of Hearing-Impaired Children and Youth reports 50,731 hearing-impaired children in programs in the United States, 7,626 of whom are of Hispanic, American Indian, Oriental, or "other" ethnic backgrounds (Center for Assessment and Demographic Studies, no date). These students comprise about 15 percent of the total population reported, not an insignificant portion.

The largest non-English-speaking language group of school-aged children is Spanish-speaking: 2.9 million of the total of 4.5 million

(Ambert & Milendez, 1985). Because of this group's size, much of the current literature is centered on the student from the Spanish-speaking home, but the concepts and problems apply to all non-English-speaking students. It is important to remember, however, that not all children from non-English-speaking homes are Hispanic. The 1980 Census revealed that within the last decade, there has been a 71.8 percent increase in the number of Native Americans (Eskimo and Aleut), a 127.6 percent increase in Asians, and a 61 percent increase in Hispanics (Ambert and Milendez, 1985).

DIVERGENT OPINIONS

Before the question of whether or not hearing-impaired children *can* become bilingual is argued, the question of the parents' desires must be considered. Such large numbers of diverse minority groups can either promote bilingual-bicultural education or inhibit it, depending on both internal and external pressures. In the first instance, if the group is eager to assimilate into the majority culture and adopt its language and customs, it will support bilingual education. On the other hand, if the group is resistant to assimilation and fears it will lose its own culture and language if it assimilates, it is likely to resist bilingual education. The interesting and contradictory aspect of this issue is that within the total group, there are likely to be factions supporting both sides of the issue (Cervantes, 1981; Lindfors, 1980; Padilla, undated; Payan, 1984; Rodriguez, 1981).

The pressures external to the group are more subtle. Economic, political, and social upward mobility are dependent on the ability to function in the language of the dominant culture, English (Kretschmer and Kretschmer, 1986). Even though the philosophical trend in education and government accepts the concept of a multicultural population, all programs promote the attainment of fluency in the dominant language (Baca and Cervantes, 1984).

The deaf community presents an interesting analogy this situation. Within the deaf population, there are those who advocate oral-aural education with the objective in mind that hearing-impaired persons should be able to integrate into the total population, and that they cannot achieve their potential intellectual, economic, and social capacities unless they have speech and language skills which will enable them to do so (Silverman, 1981; Silverman, Lane, and Calvert, 1978). Opposing this group are those who feel that the deaf can lead productive and happy lives within their own culture, the "Deaf Community," and need not be proficient in oral language skills, and that those hearing persons who are truly interested in the deaf can and will learn the deaf's esoteric language, the various forms of manual communication.

Members of the deaf community feel secure within that culture, which has its own mores, language, prohibitions, and social structure. Although the culture seems to be a "closed system" in some respects, (for example, there is very little marriage outside the group), it is not a static culture; it does respond to various political, social, and economic pressures (Schein, 1978; National Information Center on Deafness, 1984). In each instance, the non-English-speaking and the manually communicating, the wishes of the parents must be honored. Here we have a "trilemma;" oral English, the home language, or manual language. And if the third possibility is chosen, which of quite a few?

The entire concept of bilingualism, or even multilingualism, so common in Europe, should not be considered a new concept to the American population. There is a historical precedent for bilingualism in the United States. As early as 1774, the Continental Congress had its documents printed in German for the benefit of the German-speaking population; laws in New Mexico were drafted in Spanish; some Federal laws were printed in French; and all laws in the Louisiana Territory were printed in French. Moreover, these groups maintained schools where the language of instruction was that of the native tongue (Ambert & Melendez, 1985). This situation was somewhat reversed during World War I when the notion of cultural assimilation was advocated. Immigrants were expected to adopt American ways, learn English, and become acculturated in all respects (Kloss, 1977).

The pendulum appears now to have swung in the opposite direction. Perhaps due to the constantly increasing influx of non-English-speaking persons over the past several decades, and the prediction that this trend has not bottomed out, the notion of a "melting pot" has, for some educators and legislators, gradually evolved into that of a "salad bowl."

EDUCATION'S RESPONSIBILITIES

As a result of the cultural and linguistic pluralsim in the United States, education, traditionally a highly valued American institution, has been required to respond to the fact that the population of the nation is not a monolithic mass, but instead consists of more than one culture, each with its own language and cultural heritage. Education found it necessary to respond to another realization: children do not learn in a monolithic fashion; some are handicapped, and they require special programs if they are to acquire any academic achievement. As a result of these two conditions, legislation has emerged which mandates services for children with limited English proficiency (LEP), or no English proficiency (NEP), and for children with any handicapping condition which impedes their learning. Title VII of the Elementary and Secondary Act of 1968

(PL 95-561) designated children with little or no English proficiency as a population that should be provided special consideration (Provenzano, 1984). Later amendments and litigation (*Lau vs. Nichols*, 1974) supported the notion that these children could not participate effectively in English-speaking classes and were therefore not receiving meaningful instruction. As for the children with special needs in order to learn, PL 94-142, signed in 1975, and Section 504 of the Rehabilitation Act of 1973 provided that all handicapped children should receive, among other advantages, a free education in the least restrictive environment (Erickson, 1984).

Education for the hearing-impaired has a long history. As early as the sixteenth century, Pedro Ponce de Leon taught a hearing-impaired youth in Spain with great success according to his reports (Bender, 1981). In the United States, free education for hearing-impaired students has been in existence since the founding in 1817 of what is now the American School for the Deaf in Hartford, Connecticut. In those times, however, the controversy of what the language of instruction should be did not arise. For reasons pertinent to each situation, the chosen language was an obvious one; Spanish and sign language, respectively. The main impact that PL 94-142 has had on the education of hearing-impaired children is that it has placed the responsibility of the education for these children directly on individual school districts, rather than on state boards of education, which generally provide funding through state legislatures rather than through local tax bases. It requires that the programs be appropriate for each individual child, and that children be placed in the least restrictive environment.

The interpretation of the least restrictive environment has been a thorny one with disagreement among administrators, educators, and parents. Some administrators and teachers have perceived the least restrictive environment as "mainstreaming," while others have perceived mainstreaming as a most restrictive situation for certain hearing-impaired children. For some of these children, to be placed in a classroom of nonhandicapped students with only a designated period or two a day for individualized instruction is most restrictive, not least restrictive. There are some, particularly teachers who are themselves hearing-impaired, who feel that if hearing-impaired students are not placed in a school exclusively for them, they are being deprived of peer relationships with other hearing-impaired students and role models of hearing-impaired adults (Rosen, 1986). In contrast, some oral educators advocate mainstreamed environments for all hearing-impaired children with losses up to 90 dB, and that all hearing-impaired children have the right to be educated in mainstream settings (Connor, 1986). Again, there is evidence of the dichotomy of thought about the assimilation or isolation of hearing-impaired individuals.

The problem is further complicated for hearing-impaired children from non-English-speaking homes, for if they have any verbal language at all, it is likely to be the language of the home, not the language of instruction. Data on the number of such students nationally are not available, but for Texas, of the 1,204 students of Hispanic-American ethnic origin, 516 (43 percent) come from homes where Spanish is the language spoken. These figures take on an entirely different meaning if they are examined by regions of the state instead of on a state-wide basis. For example, in the south Texas region, which includes 23 Regional Schools for the Deaf where the concentration of Hispanics is the greatest, the percentage is almost half (45 percent), and in Laredo, on the Texas-Mexican border, 100 percent of the students are of Hispanic-American origin, and Spanish is the language of over 84 percent of the homes (Center for Assessment and Demographic Studies, no date). Texas has a higher concentration of students from Spanish-speaking homes than most states, and yet, even with this large large population, it has proved difficult to provide an "appropriate" program for this group of handicapped children.

AN APPROPRIATE PROGRAM

I have reported a great deal of background information to emphasize the gravity of the problem of two handicapping conditions: hearing impairment and a non-English-speaking environment. In addition, many children suffer even a third handicapping condition; poverty, a culture in and of itself (DeBlassie, 1976; Grant, 1983). This culture, too, has its own mores and prohibitions. These conditons take on extra importance with the young children who are our focus of attention here; we want to provide the best possible conditions for them in their endeavor to acquire communication competence, and each of these conditions is a powerful obstacle which must be overcome if they are to achieve success.

What would constitute an appropriate program for hearing-impaired children from non-English-speaking homes that would comply with both the Bilingual Education Act and the Education for all Handicapped Children? First of all, we would need teachers who are qualified both as teachers of hearing-impaired children and as bilingual teachers. At the present time, this would mean that teachers would be required to obtain two separate certifications or endorsements. It is possible that this extra requirement might reduce the already critically small number of qualified teachers in each area.

We would need assessment instruments that are sensitive to both conditions; hearing impairment and limited or non-Engish proficiency. There are instruments designed especially for students in each category, but to my knowledge, there are no instruments designed for this minority within a minority. Although there are tests with Spanish language versions, their validity and accuracy have been questioned by some (Ambert and

Melendez, 1985; DeAvila & Havassy, 1974; Sabatino, Kelling, and Hayden, 1973). Moreover, typical tests to ascertain children's language dominance are intended for children who have a functioning verbal system, although perhaps with some confusion as to which language is appropriate at any particular time (for example, the James Language Dominance Test [James, 1974]). Such a test would be of no value in assessing the language dominance of most young hearing-impaired children, who have little, and in many cases, no observable verbal language. Yet PL 94-142 mandates that all handicapped children be provided with nondiscriminatory assessment and evaluation with no single measurement serving as the criterion for diagnosis and placement. The regulations state further that ordinary tests used for nonhandicapped children are not necessarily appropriate (Federal Register, August 23, 1977). Consider how valid any assessment is if the child does not understand what the task is, either because of limited language proficiency or limited language generally.

Another need would be for special materials: for older children, text books, workbooks, library books; for preschool children, records, song books, story books, all printed materials in the home language of the students. In general, major publishing houses have not addressed the needs of bilingual programs (Bergin, 1980). There are now some materials designed for bilingual or English as a second language (ESL) programs, but these materials are intended mainly for children who have verbal symbols to represent basic concepts, although not in English. Preschool hearing-impaired children typically have few labels for the concepts that they have, and therefore the materials usually are not appropriate for them. For this reason, many of the materials used by teachers of hearing-impaired children are teacher-made or revised commercial materials.

In order for any educational program to succeed, it must have parental and community support. The concept of parental support for handicapped children, especially hearing-impaired children, has long been advocated and explicated throughout this volume (Grant, 1972; Luterman, 1979; Simmons-Martin and Calvert, 1978; Tracy, 1984), and PL 94-142 requires parental approval, implying parental support (Bergin, 1980). The importance of parent participation in bilingual programs has been noted also (Blanco, 1977). However, the parents of minority children have traditionally been unrepresented in parent participation in educational, social, or support-type school activities (Peters and Stephanson, 1979; Zigler, 1972). As noted, there is disagreement among professionals and nonprofessionals, including legislators and parents, as to the type of program best suited for hearing-impaired children, as well as disagreement as to the value of bilingual education. If the professionals disagree on these important issues, it might be difficult to garner strong parental and community support for any particular program. However, for a program to achieve success, total community support must be generated from school administrators, legislators, school boards, political action groups, local governments, the news media, and any institutions that have the power to influence public opinion.

PROGRAM VARIATIONS

From the above list, one might assume that the task of providing adequate services for this very special group of students is an impossible one. However, it is our charge as educators to do so. If we examine what options there are, and what attempts are being made to resolve the difficulties, we can gain some insight into the problem and suggest some strategies.

There are several philosophies as to the most advantageous approach to educating children of limited or non-English proficiency. According to definition, a bilingual program must have instruction in two languages, one of which must be English, and the study of the history and culture of the mother tongue must be included in the curriculum (U.S. Office of Education, 1971). This definition would preclude monolingual English as a Second Language programs (ESL). In ESL programs, children receive all academic instruction in a self-contained English-speaking classroom, and are "pulled out" for a certain period of time for instruction in the English language. This instruction is usually a concentrated, surface structure-type program, often labeled "audio-lingual," which requires the student to repeat sentences until the syntax and phonology become "automatic." There is little attention paid to deep structure or concept development (Lindfors, 1980). Such programs are maintained because of many factors, including the children's linguistic abilities, available funding, availability of qualified teachers, among other concerns (Ambert & Melendez, 1985). The success of these programs is equivocal, with research reports both supporting the programs and criticizing them (The American Institutes of Research, 1978; Baker and deKanter, 1981, Swain, 1979; Willig, 1982). From this description, it would appear that an ESL program would do little to advance concept development, deep structure, or the acquisition of language for young hearing-impaired children. Teachers of hearing-impaired children have long since rejected programs of this type as ineffective in developing usable communication skills.

Truly bilingual programs, those in which instruction is in two languages, fall along a continuum so far as philosophies and objectives are concerned. To delineate and describe them fully here is not possible or necessary. Suffice it to say that they range from transitional programs to maintenance programs. In the former, the principle objective is to advance the students to the point that they can achieve academically through English instruction only. This type of program is the choice of the group that feels that assimilation into the majority culture is the goal. Normally, students are retained in such programs for a specified period of time, usually three years, during which time, academic subject instruction in English is introduced gradually, one subject at a time.

In contrast, the aim of maintenance programs, the preferred type for the group which advocates a pluralistic education and society, is for students to learn in two languages and maintain proficiency in both languages. Advocates of maintenance programs are concerned primarily with cognitive and affective growth which they feel is fostered by the ability to think in two languages (Baca and Cervantes, 1984; Blanco, 1977). Obviously, maintenance programs require a greater commitment of personnel, funding, and energy than transitional ones, and therefore are less prevalent.

Most of the research reported here concerns normally hearing elementary aged students. The problem is more acute with preschool aged children, and when the problem is compounded by a hearing impairment, it has additional ramifications. These are the resonant years for learning language, and children are predisposed to acquire a language (deVilliers & deVilliers, 1978). What is more, they will learn whatever language they are exposed to. If they are not exposed to a verbal language or a formal manual language, they will devise one; somehow they will communicate (Blackwell and Fischgrund, 1984). Normally hearing children will acquire two languages during these years if they receive sufficient exposure; we can only speculate whether or not hearing-impaired children can do likewise.

Education of the hearing impaired, like bilingual education, has a continuum of types of programs, each with a cadre of supporters with strong biases. At one pole are the oral-auralists, who maintain that through this method hearing-impaired students can gain the skills that will permit them to be mainstreamed and enable them to function successfully with their nonhandicapped peers (Northcott, 1981). At the other end of the continuum is exclusive manualism, the use of American Sign Language (ASL). This is the preferred language of the deaf community mentioned earlier and has attained the status of a complete language in and of itself, not "an ungrammatical version of English" (Rosen, 1986, p. 246). Although this status is questioned by some (Schlesinger and Namir, 1979), it is confirmed by other researchers (Klima and Bellugi, 1979; Stokoe, 1972; Wilbur, 1979). However, no programs ignore the teaching of English entirely, and all programs give at least lip service to the development of speech skills for hearing-impaired children (Moores, 1982).

In between these two poles lies total communication. There are a number of forms of total communication, and usually they are some form of English in a manual code, as opposed to ASL, although most systems use ASL hand configurations. There are, to name a few, Manually Coded English, Seeing Essential English (SEE I), Seeing Essential English (SEE II),

Signed English and Pidgin Sign English (Quigley and Paul, 1984). In addition, some schools or districts have developed their own systems; for example, in Texas a manually coded English system entitled *Preferred signs for Instructional Purposes* (Texas Education Agency, 1982) is used in all the Regional Schools for the Deaf. The preferred choice of communication in most programs for hearing-impaired children, in the United States is some form of manual communication (Connor, 1986), but there is no consensus as to the "best" system.

The important point here is that more often than not, one of these forms of communication is the first or "native language" of many hearing-impaired children, no matter what the language of the home is. Its resemblance to or difference from English plays an important role in the language acquisition process of hearing-impaired children from non-English-speaking homes. For if English or ASL is the first language the child has, and the home language is neither, the child is facing a problem similar to that of the normally hearing student who has English at school and another language at home.

It is difficult to make generalizations about the appropriate programs for any hearing-impaired children, much less those from non-English-speaking homes. There are so many variables which influence a child's progress. A hearing-impaired child's success at acquiring language will depend on the degree and configuration of the hearing impairment, the age at which amplification was initiated, the age of entry into a program, the parental wishes, the parental support, the child's motivation to communicate, as well as intelligence and socioeconomic status (which correlate positively with language acquisition) (Quigley, 1986).

There is a great difference, however, between the normally hearing and the hearing-impaired child from the non-English-speaking home in that many of the latter group enter programs with no appreciable verbal language. This does not mean that these children cannot communicate; many of them have highly developed nonverbal communication systems (Blackwell and Fischgrund, 1984; Golden-Meadow and Mylander, 1984). What it means is that they have no verbal system upon which they are building verbal communication competence as the normally hearing child is in his home language. They (hearing-impaired children) learn English, signed English, or ASL at school, and build linguistic competence on that system. But for children from non-English-speaking homes, none of these is the home language. Thus, such a child is faced with the problem of acquiring one language at school and another language at home. In other words, he must, by default, become bilingual if he is to succeed at school and communicate at home.

Some time ago, I interviewed a hearing-impaired child and her parents from Laredo, a city on the Texas-Mexico border. This bright, beautiful, five-year-old girl was gleefully demonstrating her fine writing and speech skills in English for me. The mother spoke no English, and the father spoke very little. I asked how many children were in the family and if any others were hearing-impaired. The father told me that this little girl was one of eight and the only one with a hearing impairment. I asked if any of them spoke English, and the response was that some spoke a little. I asked what language was used at home, and the father was surprised at my asking and answered Spanish. No one in the family signed although the little girl was learning *Preferred Signs for Instructional Purposes.* With whom was this child to communicate in her own family? This incident occurred some time ago, but the situation is not much improved now. There is no formal plan to accommodate hearing-impaired children from non-English-speaking homes in Texas, although the problem is at least recognized today. Depending on the available bilingual personnel, the degree of hearing impairment the child has, and the wishes of the parents, instruction and communication in the various programs are in whatever form is most expedient. This is not to imply the administrations, both local and state, are not sympathetic to the problem, but in the absence of an overall plan and adequately trained personnel, there is a lack of consistency in the educational programs of these children (P. Archer, personal communication, June 15, 1986).

RESOLVING THE PROBLEM

What are some possible solutions to this serious problem? If we examine the outlined obstacles to bilingual programs for hearing-impaired children, perhaps we can conceive at least partial solutions to the situation. The listed requirements—qualified personnel, appropriate assessment and evaluation instruments, ample materials, and parental and community support—were not listed in any special order. It would be hard to determine which of these items should be considered prime, and this list is not comprehensive, only representative. Instead, it might be more expeditious to order the list in a logical sequence, attending to what must precede what.

Community support, that is *community* in the generic sense, is a starting point. By community, I mean all its institutions; legislatures, school districts, local governments, religious organizations, health services, social services, news media, and parent groups, all institutions that affect the lives of children. The legislation is already in place, and many school districts have complied to the best of their abilities. However, the legislation addresses the issues separately—children with hearing impairments and children of limited or no English proficiency—it does not address the combined problem that we face. Moreover, there is that third problem to contend with; poverty. There is no legislation that prohibits poverty, and we have evidence that socioeconomic status is an influencing factor in academic achievement (Quigley, 1986).

Under ordinary circumstances, the group that probably could exert the most influence to establish bilingual programs for hearing-impaired children would be the parents. However, as noted previously, these parents are likely to be living in poverty, worrying about food and clothing for their children. Generally, they speak little or no English and thus are not likely to instigate the action required. Therefore, it is up to the others, the educators, the school administrators, and the school boards, to do what is necessary to create the environment where these children can learn and become productive citizens.

My experience with these parents has been that they are most eager and cooperative in supporting school programs, but they are often intimidated by all professionals, politicians, and English-speaking people in general. However, if they are approached in their own language and encouraged to act, they can be effective promoters of adequate and appropriate educational programs for their children, and can become active participants, themselves, in the educational process of their children (Schaeffer-Dressler, 1981). In Texas, any actions or proposed actions concerning a handicapped child must be communicated to the parents in their home language. It is usually written, but if this is not feasible (e.g., if the parents are illiterate), other means must be used. This requirement is spelled out very clearly in the *Texas Administrative Code* (Texas Education Agency, no date). The mechanisms for parental support are in place; all that is needed is a catalyst to spur the parents into action.

The implications here for hearing-impaired infants and young children is obvious. The parent–infant facilitator and the preschool teacher must develop a cooperative arrangement with the parents, and this is most difficult, if not impossible, to do through an interpreter. This problem brings us to the next obstacle on the list; qualified personnel. Ideally, we would have native speakers in all the various professional roles that impact on hearing-impaired children: teachers, audiologists, speech pathologists, school administrators, otologists, social workers. Lacking that ideal situation, it would be most helpful if we had even bilingual teachers. Most universities expend concerted efforts to recruit minority students. However, at many universities, often the Mexican-American students who can meet the standards for admission are very middle-class, not representative of the lower socioeconomic levels, and often not even bilingual. These students are not members of the culture that most of the hearing-impaired children from Spanish-speaking homes represent. To recruit students from the lower socioeconomic levels will likely require substantial financial assistance.

Students in all accredited teacher education programs become sensitized to the difficulties encountered by both handicapped children and linguistically and culturally different children; these requirements are stated in the standards of the National Council for Accreditation of Teacher Education (NCATE). In addition, teacher education programs are encouraged to have as members of their faculties minority personnel

(NCATE, 1982). However, this requirement and encouragement does not provide bilingual personnel for classrooms. What is needed are programs to prepare teachers, parent–infant facilitators, supervisors, and administrators for hearing-impaired children from non-English-speaking homes. A possible solution would be for a university which offers a program for teachers of hearing-impaired children and one for bilingual teachers to combine its resources to provide adequate preparation for this sub-specialty group. Inservice options are among other possibilities (Grant, 1984). There are a few bilingual parent–infant facilitators in Texas, but not enough to serve all the non-English-speaking families. In other states and regions, and in Texas too, there are other non-English-speaking groups of children beside Spanish-speaking, and often the number is so small that it is impossible to find personnel who can properly serve these hearing-impaired children and their families.

What about materials? As mentioned, there are some bilingual materials available on the market, but not in great abundance. However, much of it is not appropriate for hearing-impaired children, and especially not for very young children, our focus here. In Texas, an effort is being made to develop materials, mostly for parents. Parts of the *Ski*Hi Curriculum Manual* (Clark and Watkins, 1985), which is the program used by parent–infant facilitators throughout the state in the regional programs, has been translated into Spanish. This translation has proved most helpful in making it possible for non-English-speaking parents to be active participants in their children's education. In addition, the *Parent Handbook* (TEA, no date) to accompany the program has a Spanish as well as an English version.

Assessment is another issue that presents special problems for hearing-impaired children from non-English-speaking homes. Again, each group, the hearing-impaired and the child of limited English proficiency, has suffered from bias in all kinds of testing situations (DeBlassie, 1980; Kopp, 1984; Oakland, 1977; Samuda, 1975; Zieziula, 1982). The same difficulties surface for each group: "The history of the assessment of hearing-impaired people shares a remarkable resemblance to that of Hispanic children" (Figueroa, Delgado, and Ruiz, 1984, p. 141). For both groups, there is a wide discrepancy between their performance abilities and their verbal abilities on any standardized tests. Mean scores for these groups are in the normal range on performance scales, but scores on verbal tests show the groups to be in the mentally retarded range. In both cases, the language deficit or difference is the culprit. According to Figueroa and colleagues (1984), there has been more progress in the assessment of bilingual students than in the area of the hearing-impaired. Their recommendation is that until there are truly suitable instruments for this population, examiners must evaluate with the unique needs of each group borne in mind and use additional strategies, such as observational study, as a supplementary means of assessing the children. This suggestion is particularly pertinent to the assessment of young hearing-impaired children as the frequent absence of verbal language misleads psychologists and other professionals to draw faulty conclusions concerning a child's intellectual capacity. Often, astute observation can tell a teacher much more about a hearing-impaired child's abilities than standardized tests.

PROGRAM OPTIONS

At present, there are not many options for services available to children and families of non-English-speaking homes. The problem is intensified by the fact that each child and each family is unique. First of all, the parents' wishes must be respected. Even if the parents wish their child to retain his culture and acquire the home language, the school is obliged to have for one of its objectives the acquisition of English; this is inherent in all bilingual programs. In such a case, it would be necessary for the child to become at least bilingual, and perhaps trilingual if ASL is part of the school curriculum. Some educators may feel that such an outcome is beyond the realm of possibility for hearing-impaired children, but according to Blackwell and Fischgrund (1984), ". . . bilingualism is as natural a linguistic and social phenomenon as monolingualism" (p. 162), and therefore we should not fear that is achievement is not feasible for hearing-impaired children. They urge that the child's home environment and language not be ignored nor dismissed even if the child seems to have no apparent verbal language; the environment of the home will still be part of the child's life. Cummings (1979) has stated that the better the child's language competence in his native language, the better will be he his competence in the second language. Cummings was not referring to hearing-impaired children, but most educators of these children strive to have them acquire language as closely as possible to the process that hearing children go through. It would be foolhardy to ignore the research that has been reported on normally hearing chlidren.

The possibility of hearing-impaired children achieving bilingualism is enhanced when the children are entered in parent–infant programs early in their lives during the critical period for language acquisition. Ideally, the children would establish competency in the home language through abundant and systematized linguistic input from the parents, appropriate amplification, and training in using their hearing. According to Cummings (1981), experiences in one language will promote efficiency in the second language. If the parents are monolingual, it is unrealistic to expect them to provide "abundant and systemized" linguistic input in English. It could be just another frustrating and depressing aspect of the (re)habilitation process if they are pressured to speak a language in which they have no fluency and no apparent need. It is entirely possible that the children could acquire the home language during the infancy and toddler years, and have enough linguistic competency to add English during the preschool years.

True, not all infants have this ideal early start, and programs have to be designed for individual families. Some parents are eager to learn English and learn along with their babies. Another strategy that holds promise is that of teaching the parents American Sign Language (ASL) but using Spanish translations instead of English. McLean (no date) has developed such materials for three levels of competency, and the response has been very positive especially in terms of improving communication between parents and schools where there are no bilingual personnel.

There is another interesting aspect to the bilingual–bicultural problem in educating hearing-impaired children. That is the hearing-impaired child of hearing-impaired parents who use ASL. These children are likely to have a highly developed language in ASL even before they enter a program. The same principles hold true here. These children's language and culture can play a very positive role in learning English, and the research has reported that such children are accelerated in language compared to hearing-impaired children of hearing parents (Meadow, 1968). We must remember, though, that less than ten percent of the hearing-impaired population have hearing-impaired parents (Rosen, 1986).

There are two noteworthy programs that have had at least a decade of experience providing bilingual–bicultural programs for hearing-impaired children: The Projecto Oportunidad at the Rhode Island School for the Deaf, and the bilingual–bicultural program at the Lexington School for the Deaf in New York. The latter was not actually initiated until 1981, but this was after six years of research on Cooperative Research Endeavors in the Education of the Deaf (CREED) (Lerman & Vila, 1984). Both these programs have emphasized the importance of using the home culture and language, not only for improved academic achievement, but for improved relations between the homes of the students and the schools, and improved self-images for both the students and their parents (Fischgrund, 1984; Lerman, 1984). Lerman and Vila (1984) speak of the need for more bilingual personnel and "the development of a core of Hispanic parents" (p.179).

SUMMARY

Educators of the hearing-impaired must realize that there exists a special problem that will not go away; if anything it will continue to grow as the influx of a non-English-speaking population increases in the United States. In order to serve these children, we need parental and public support, adequately prepared personnel, appropriate assessment instruments, and ample materials. The two programs in Rhode Island and New York need to be replicated, and their success needs to be exploited. Americans have always cherished their children and wanted the best for them. We must not neglect any segment of the population simply because they are a small percentage of the total; each child deserves to develop to his maximum potential.

REFERENCES

Ambert, A. and Melendez, S. (1985). *Bilingual education: A sourcebook.* New York: Garland Publishing.

American Institutes for Research. (1978). *Evaluation of the impact of ESEA Title VII Spanish/English bilingual programs.* Los Angeles: National Dissemination and Assessment Center, California State University.

Baca, L. and Cervantes, H. (1984). *The bilingual special education interface.* St. Louis: Times Mirror/Mosby College Publishing.

Baker, K. and deKanter, A. (1981). The effectiveness of bilingual education: A review of the literature. *Final Draft Report to the U.S. Department of Education, Office of Planning, Budget, and Evaluation. (ERIC Document Reproduction Service No. ED 215 010).*

Bender, R. (1981). *The conquest of deafness.* Danville, IL: The Interstate Printers.

Bergin, V. (1980). *Special education needs in bilingual programs.* Rosslyn, VA.: National Clearing House for Bilingual Education.

Blackwell, P. and Fischgrund, J. (1984). Issues in the development of culturally responsive programs for deaf students from nonEnglish-speaking homes. In G. Delgado (Ed.), *The Hispanic deaf.* Washington, DC: Gallaudet College Press.

Blanco, G. (1977). The education perspective. In *Bilingual education: Current perspectives.* Arlington, VA: Center for Applied Linguistics.

Center for Assessment and Demographic Studies. (no date). *1984–85 Annual survey of hearing impaired children and youth.* Gallaudet College, Washington, D.C.

Cervantes, R. (1981). Bilingual education: The best of times, the worst of times. In K. Coles-Cirincione (Ed.), *The future of education: Policy issues and challenges.* Los Angeles: Sage Publications.

Clark, T. and Watkins, S. (1985). *SkiʹHi curriculum manual.* Logan, UT: Department of Communication Disorders, State University of Utah.

Connor, L. (1986). Oralism in perspective. In D. Luterman (Ed.), *Deafness in perspective.* San Diego: College-Hill Press.

Cummings, J. (1979). Linguistic interdependence and the educational development of bilingual children. *Review of Educational Research, 49,* 222–251.

Cummings, J. (1981). Four misconceptions about language proficiency in bilingual education. *NABE Journal, 5,* 31–45.

DeAvila, E. and Havassy, B. (1974). The testing of minority children: A neo-Piagetian approach. *Today's Education, 63,* 72–75.

DeBlassie, R. (1976). *Counseling with Mexican American youth: Preconceptions and processes.* Austin, TX: Learning Concepts.

DeBlassie, R. (1980). *Testing Mexican American youth.* Hingham, MA: Teaching Resources.

de Villiers, J. and de Villiers, P. (1978). *Language acquisition.* Cambridge, MA: Harvard University Press.

Erickson , J. (1984). Hispanic deaf children: A bilingual and special education challenge. In G. Delgado (Ed.), *The Hispanic deaf.* Washington, DC: Gallaudet College Press.

Federal Register, August 22, 1977, p. 42494.

Figueroa, R., Delgado, G., and Ruiz, N. (1984). Assessment of Hispanic children: Implications for Hispanic hearing impaired children. In G. Delgado (Ed.), *The Hispanic deaf.* Washington, DC: Gallaudet College Press.

Fischgrund, J. (1984). Language intervention for hearing impaired children from linguistically and culturally diverse backgrounds. In G. Delgado (Ed.), *The Hispanic deaf.* Washington, DC: Gallaudet College Press.

Goldin-Meadow, S. and Mylander, C. (1984). Gestural communication in deaf children: The effects and noneffects of parental input on early language development. *Monographs of the Society for Research in Child Development, 49*(3–4, Serial No. 207).

Grant, J. (1972). *Proceedings of a workshop on the preparation of personnel in education of bilingual hearing impaired children, ages 0–4.* San Antonio, TX: Trinity University.

Grant, J. (1983). The bilingual hearing impaired: Teaching children and preparing teachers. In D. Omark and J. Erickson (Eds.), *The bilingual exceptional child.* San Diego: College-Hill Press.

Grant, J. (1984). Teachers of Hispanic hearing impaired children: Competencies and preparation. In G. Delgado (Ed.), *The Hispanic deaf.* Washington, DC: Gallaudet College Press.

James, P. (1974). *James language dominance test: English/Spanish.* Austin, TX: Learning Concepts.

Klima, E. and Bellugi, U. (1979). *The signs of language.* Cambridge, MA: Harvard University Press.

Kloss, H. (1977). *The American bilingual tradition.* Rowley, MA: Newbury House.

Kopp, H. (1984). Bilingual problems of the Hispanic deaf. In G. Delgado (Ed.), *The Hispanic deaf.* Washington, DC: Gallaudet College Press.

Kretschmer, R. and Kretschmer, L. (1986). Language in perspective. In D. Luterman (Ed.), *Deafness in perspective.* San Diego: College-Hill Press.

Lau v. Nichols, (1974). 414 U.S. 563;39L. Ed2nd 1, 94 S. Ct. 786.

Lerman, A. (1984). Survey of Hispanic hearing-imapired students and their families in New York City. In G. Delgado (Ed.), *The Hispanic deaf.* Washington, DC: Gallaudet College Press.

Lerman, A. and Vila, C. (1984). A model for school services to Hispanic hearing impaired children. In G. Delgado (Ed.), *The Hispanic deaf.* Washington, DC: 1984.

Lindfors, J. (1980). *Children's language and learning.* Englewood Cliffs, NJ: Prentice-Hall.

Luterman, D. (1979). *Counseling parents of hearing impaired children.* Boston: Little, Brown.

McLean, M. (no date). *La communicacion de los sordos.* Austin, TX: Texas School for the Deaf.

Meadow, K. (1968). Early manual communication in relation to the deaf child's intellectual, social, and communicative functioning. *American Annals of the Deaf, 113,* 29–41.

Moores, D. (1982). *Educating the deaf.* Boston: Houghton Mifflin.

National Advisory Council for Bilingual Education. (1981). *The prospects for bilingual education in the nation* (NACBE Fifth Annual Report, 1980–81). Washington, DC: Author.

National Council for Accreditation of Teacher Education. (1982). *Standards for the accreditation of teacher education.* Washington, DC: Author.

National Informaton Center on Deafness. (1984). Deafness; a fact sheet. In *Information packet on bilingual education.* Washington, DC: National Clearing House for Bilingual Education.

Northcott, W. (1981). Freedom through speech: Every child's right. *Volta Review, 83,* 162–181.

Oakland, T. (Ed.). (1977). *Psychological and educational assessment of minority children.* New York: Brunner/Mazel.

Padilla, R. (undated). *A theoretical framework for the analysis of bilingual education policy formation.* (ERIC Document Reproduction Service No. ED 217 719)

Payan, R. (1984). Development of the bilingual special education interface. In L. Baca and H. Cervantes (Eds.), *The bilingual special education interface.* St. Louis: Times Mirror/Mosby College.

Peters, N. and Stephanson, W. (Winter, 1979). Parents as partners in a program for children with oral language and readiness disabilities. *Teaching Exceptional Children,* 64–65.

Provenzano, J. (1984). *Guide to Title VII.* Rosslyn, VA: National Clearing House for Bilingual Education.

Quigley, S. (1986). A perspective on academic achievement. In D. Luterman (Ed.), *Deafness in perspective.* San Diego: College-Hill Press.

Quigley, S. and Paul, P. (1984). *Language and deafness.* San Diego: College-Hill Press.

Rodriguez, R. (1981). *Hunger of memory: The education of Richard Rodriguez.* Boston: David R. Godine.

Rosen, R. (1986). Deafness: A social perspective. In D. Luterman (Ed.), *Deafness in perspective.* San Diego: College-Hill Press.

Sabatino, D., Kelling, K., and Hayden, D. (1973). Special education and the culturally different child: Implications for assessment and intervention. *Exceptional Children, 39,* 563–567.

Samuda, R. (1975). *Psychological testing of American minorities: Issues and consequences.* New York: Dodd, Mead.

Schaeffer-Dresler, P. (1981). *Hearing impaired children from Spanish speaking homes.* Unpublished master's thesis, California State University, Los Angeles.

Schein, J. (1978). The deaf community. In H. Davis and S. Silverman, (Eds.), *Hearing and deafness.* New York: Holt, Rinehart, and Winston.

Schlesinger, I. and Namir, L. (Eds.). (1978). *Sign language of the deaf.* New York: Academic Press.

Silverman, S. (1981). Mainstreaming: Update—1960–1980 in the United States.

In R. Bender, *The conquest of deafness*. Danville, IL: The Interstate Printers and Publishers.

Silverman, S., Lane, H., and Calvert, D. (1978). Early and elementary education. In H. Davis and S. Silverman (Eds.), *Hearing and deafness*. New York: Holt, Rinehart, and Winston.

Simmons-Martin, A., and Calvert, D. (Eds.). (1978). *Parent/infant intervention: Communication disorders*. New York: Grune & Stratton.

Standardization of Signs Committee for Schools of the Deaf in Texas. (1982). *Preferred Signs for Instructional Purposes*. Austin, TX: Texas Education Agency, 1982.

Stokoe, W. (1972). *Semiotics and human sign languages*. The Hague: Mouton.

Swain, M. (1979). Bilingual education: Research and its implications. In C. Yorio, K. Perkinds, and J. Schacter (Eds.), *ON TESOL '79: The learner in focus*. Washington, DC: TESOL.

Texas Education Agency. (no date). *Parent handbook*. Austin, TX: Author.

Texas Education Agency. (No date). *Texas administrative code #89.229 (c)*. Austin, TX: Author.

Tracy, L. (1984). *Talks to parents*. Los Angeles: Jeffries Banknote.

U.S. Office of Education. (1971). *Programs under the bilingual education act. Manual for project applicants and grantees*. Washington, DC: Government Printing Office.

Wilbur, R. (1979). *American sign language and sign systems*. Baltimore: University Park Press.

Willig, A. (1982). The effectiveness of bilingual education: Review of a report. *NABE Journal, 2*, 1–19.

Zieziula, F. (1982). *Assessment of hearing-impaired people*. Washington, DC: Gallaudet College Press.

Zigler, E. (December, 1972). Child care in the 70's. In *Inequality in Education*. Cambridge, MA: Harvard Center for Law and Education, No. 13.

CHAPTER 10

Epilogue

A s stated in the Preface, this book was not intended to be a cook-
book, one that the teacher would grab to get an inspiration of what
to present on Monday morning; instead, it was intended to offer some
ideas to be contemplated and pondered. It is my notion that teachers must
have a philosophy, a system of principles that shape their thoughts about
teaching and learning and guide them in classroom procedures. It is my
hope that this volume has offered some new insights that perhaps had not
occurred to the reader. Above all, I hope that every reader comes away
with the conviction that hearing-impaired children *can* learn a verbal
language, and they can learn to use it to their great advantage.

Because language is learned and not taught, teachers and parents will
have to create environments whereby this process can take place. Parent–
infant facilitators will have to convince parents that the process can evolve
with their support, and it is up to the parent–infant facilitators to show
the way. Teachers may find themselves doing what should have been done
in the home a few years earlier in the cases of hearing-impaired children
who had not been identified at the optimal time, early infancy. The
variation in the time of identification, alone, should convince teachers of
each child's uniqueness and the tremendous implications for management.
Consider also, the wide variation in degree and configuration of the
impairment, intelligence, socioeconomic background, temperament, and
parental support. No two children are going to share identical patterns
in any of these characteristics. Even children with what appears to be
similar or identical puretone audiograms will develop quite differently in

their abilities to use their hearing. The teacher, every day, is offered convincing proof of the individual differences of each student; her preparations must reflect these differences if she is to serve each child effectively.

Experienced teachers are sure to notice the lack of mention of the child who does not learn like the rest of the children, the child with other handicapping conditions, or the child who defies all efforts to make learning the natural path it should be. These children, more than the others, need the approach advocated here; first hand experiences, varied experiences, uniting all the stimuli into an integrated whole, the global approach to assist the child in developing concepts from which he can induce principles and generalizatons. If it is important for the bright and gifted child to be stimulated and exposed to varied and exciting experiences, it is all the more important for the child who is mentally retarded, has emotional disorders, learning disabilities, or undefinable problems, to receive these same considerations. We must remember that all children can learn, although the going may be slow and arduous for some.

Teachers, like their students, are unique, and every good teacher intuitively develops individual strategies and approaches for dealing with the various personalities of her students. As Jarvis states (1986), a teacher can discover the key to each child's personality and learning style by observing what he says, does, draws, and plays. Some children seem to resist divulging what their problems are, but the astute teacher will note the channels through which the child reveals his idiosyncratic behavior and use the knowledge as a guide to promote learning. Every child is worth whatever extra effort it takes to solve his learning problems, no matter how obscure.

The business of instructing parents has been discussed as if all parents were most eager, cooperative, and able to carry out all the instructions and admonitions of the parent–infant facilitator. That, of course, is not always the case. It sometimes appears as if some parents are completely unconcerned about the welfare and education of their children. Such parents may exist, but most parents want the best possible situations for their children, and often the parents who appear to be recalcitrant are, in reality, only unknowledgeable or timorous. Many such parents can become vigorous partners in their child's education by nonpatronizing instruction and genuine compassion on the part of teachers and administrators. Parents, like the children and their teachers, are unique individuals and as such, each expresses herself or himself in a unique fashion. Professionals can glean insight into the best approach to each family by observing, listening, and acknowledging the opinions and wishes of its members.

I would hope that every teacher of hearing-impaired children would consider herself an advocate for all hearing-impaired persons, from infants to adults. This advocacy includes informing other educators, one's friends and acquaintances, and the public at large if the opportunity presents itself, of the capabilities of hearing-impaired persons. The world should know that hearing-impairment is a physical impairment with a communication involvement, not a mental handicap. Although special educational procedures are necessary, hearing-impaired persons possess the same potential for intellectual development as the total population. At this time, with rapid technological and surgical advances taking place, the educational, economic, and social opportunities are greater than they have ever been. As yet, sensorineural deafness cannot be "cured," but until that miracle happens, let us endeavor to make it possible for each child to develop all his endowments to the fullest.

REFERENCES

Jarvis, K. (1986). A teacher's quest for a child's questions. *Harvard Educational Review, 56,* 132–150.

Author Index

Subject Index

Italic page numbers refer to figures.

A

Audiologist, role in intervention, 93
Auditory activities, importance in
    early education, 90–92

B

Bilingualism, and hearing-impaired
    children,
    appropriate personnel for, 151
    assessment considerations, 151–153
    educational legislation, 149–150
    educational programs, 153–156
      implementation, 156–159
      options, 159–160
    parents' role, 157
    social pressures, 148–149
Brain function, models, 28–29

C

Chart story, use in early education
    programs, 123–124, *125*
Cognitive development stages in
    children, 31–32

Computers, use in instructional
    programs, 140–144, *142,*
    144
    LOGO language use, 142–144
Counseling needs, of parents of
    hearing-impaired children,
    83–85
Creative expression, in instructional
    programs, 133–134
    computers use, 140–144, *142,*
    144
    language and, 139–140
    music and dance, 138–139
    symbolic and dramatic play,
      137–138
    visual and plastic arts, 135–136,
      135

D

Dramatic play, in instructional
    programs, 137–138

E

Early education programs,
    adaptation for hearing-impaired
      children, 111–118
    cognitive growth, 101–102
    logical thinking, 100–101,
      101, 115–118, *116*